Napkin Notes: On the Art of Living
by
Gary Michael Durst, Ph.D.

Center for the Art of Living
Evanston, Illinois
1982

Reprinted 1982

For information address:

The Center for the Art of Living,
P.O. Box 788,
Evanston, Illinois 60204

Library of Congress
Catalog Card Number
79-50554

ISBN: 0-9602552-2-2 (Trade ed.)

"My task which I am trying to achieve is, by the power of the written word, to make you hear, to make you feel -- it is, before all, to make you see. That -- and no more -and it is everything. If I succeed, you shall find there... encouragement, consolation, fear, charm, all you demand -and, perhaps, also that glimpse of truth for which you have forgotten to ask."

-- Joseph Conrad

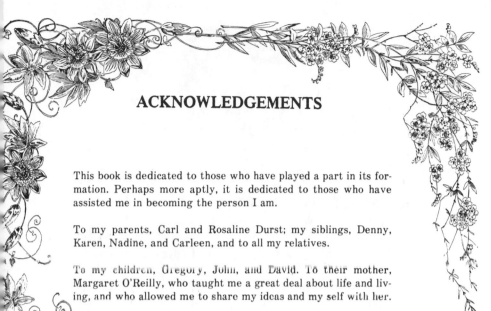

ACKNOWLEDGEMENTS

This book is dedicated to those who have played a part in its formation. Perhaps more aptly, it is dedicated to those who have assisted me in becoming the person I am.

To my parents, Carl and Rosaline Durst; my siblings, Denny, Karen, Nadine, and Carleen, and to all my relatives.

To my children, Gregory, John, and David. To their mother, Margaret O'Reilly, who taught me a great deal about life and living, and who allowed me to share my ideas and my self with her.

To my best friend, F. Stephen Barick, whose encouragement and support manifested itself in this book. Through him I have learned of acceptance and love, of trust and joy.

To my friends and the graduates of my programs, all of whom have taught me, nurtured me, and served me.

To my teachers and guides. To my early mentors: Mrs. Laverne Johnson, J. D. Dellinger, Jane and Joe Palmer, John Eddy, and Roberta Christi. To my guides in print, who, through their words, were able to share a view of life I could experience from within: Eric Berne, Abraham Maslow, Carl Rodgers, Fritz Pearls, Alan Watts, Carlos Castaneda, and R. D. Laing. To my living teachers: Werner Erhard, for getting me in touch with cause; Bhagwan Shree Rajneesh, for putting everything into context and for providing the blank verse format for this book. To my religious guides, whose words and teachings become more alive daily. Jesus Christ, Lao Tzu, and Buddha.

And to me: for having written these napkin notes and for having the courage to publish them, in hopes that these thoughts will serve others in their journey.

NAPKIN NOTES: ON THE ART OF LIVING IS ABOUT YOU.

Its purpose is to allow you to become aware of your ability to experience responsibility, satisfaction, and success in your life.

The book is written in free verse; it is not a book to "speed read." Reflect upon the words. Create your own sense of what they mean. "Fill in the blanks" with your own experience.

A Zen master begins his sessions by stating, "Imagine that I'm only talking directly and solely to you." Likewise, to gain maximum value, imagine that this book was written expressly for you.

Much of the philosophy contained within these pages is shared during a three-day seminar called, "Management By Responsibility," and a weekend, personal training called "The Art of Living." This book is not intended to replace those trainings. However, if you allow yourself to experience these words, you can create your own training. Your life will allow you to practice taking charge and determining your own direction.

When education is meaningful it produces change. Simple awareness does not produce change. You produce change. Awareness only gives you a choice. This book will best serve you by increasing your awareness, so that you may choose to change. If this book only becomes one more in a series of "self-help" books, seminars, and lectures, it has failed in its purpose. If it assists you by increasing your knowledge of self and expanding your options, it has succeeded in its mission.

Napkin Notes: On the Art of Living is a culmination of my life experiences.

As a teacher, counselor, administrator, and management trainer, I noticed one recurring theme. People were always blaming others for their negative experiences.

And yet, it was the blaming that kept everyone stuck. Supporting such an "effect" position ("They're doing it to me") only masked the symptoms of the underlying problem. The problem was the unwillingness on the part of most people to take responsibility for their own experience. Eliminating one symptom simply led to the creation of another.

PLAYING LIFE FROM EFFECT

When we say, "I don't like it"; i.e. when we feel angry, upset, frustrated, embarrassed, or "put down," we play from an "effect" position. "They did it to me," whether it was my spouse, my boss, the economy, or the weather. We tend to take no responsibility, and feel as though we had no choice in the matter.

However, when we say, "I liked it," whatever "it" was, we play from a cause position. "I did it to me" is generally what we acknowledge: I worked overtime, I chose to take this vacation, I finished the family room. If we like what is occurring in our experience we tend to take total, 100% responsibility and we assume that we had total choice:

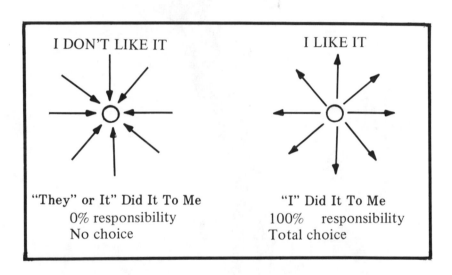

I DON'T LIKE IT

I LIKE IT

"They" or It" Did It To Me
0% responsibility
No choice

"I" Did It To Me
100% responsibility
Total choice

The truth is simple: we are responsible for everything in our experience, whether we like it or not. Liking or not liking the situation are only evaluations. These same evaluations often change with time. Individuals typically report upon reflection that what they deemed to be negative was the perfect experience for them.

We've all been taught very successfully to play life from an effect position, and to avoid responsibility. This book assumes just the opposite. Its very point of view runs counter to much of Western thought. Indeed our very language is an "effect" language. Listen to all the phrases: "You made me angry," "You hurt my feelings," "The time ran out," "She left me high and dry," "My boss frustrates the hell out of me."

If you turn on the radio or TV you can hear and see dramatic examples of effect positions. I have a friend who collects examples of what he calls "Country Western Effect Songs." These include such titles as, "You Stole My Heart and Stomped That Sucker Flat" and "If This Ain't Thanksgivin', Why Am I Stuck With a Turkey Like You?" Our society supports an effect position, both socially and politically.

IF THIS AIN'T THANKSGIVING, WHY AM I STUCK WITH A TURKEY LIKE YOU?

The corollary problem is equally as devastating. People involved with the human potential movement often use therapy and group experiences to support the opposite "effect" position. In other words, instead of saying that something or someone was "doing it to them," they would wait for something or someone to "do it *for* them."

People would wait for their therapist to "help" them or hope that a training would make their life work better. Many became addicted to Transactional Analysis, est, Gestalt, rolfing, psychoanalysis, transcendental meditation, assertiveness training, and primal scream therapy. Few had heeded Alan Watts' admonishment that if you see a signpost that says "New York," climbing the post won't get you anywhere. Signs only point you in the right direction. All trainings, including my own, can only point you in the right direction.

In order for any of those experiences to have meaning, one needs to assume that position of "cause." Otherwise, you're constantly searching for the latest, the best, the most wonderful experience, and then feeling frustration because the effects don't last.

IN BASEBALL, IT'S THE WIND UP AND THE PITCH, IN LIFE, IT'S OFTEN THE SET-UP AND THE BITCH.

IN BASEBALL, IT'S THE WIND UP AND THE PITCH, IN LIFE, IT'S OFTEN THE SET-UP AND THE BITCH.

You are the one who makes your life work. *You* are the one who gets it all together not someone or something else.

To assume that you're the cause of your experience goes to the root, the basis, the heart of the matter. To do so is to allow change to take place without efforting, working at it, or trying to make it happen. Assuming a cause position enables you to take charge and to see the perfection of you.

It's as though you never escape the Truth you already know. That's my experience. Aspects of the truth about how life works would become apparent in the strangest places at the strangest times. That's why this book is called, *Napkin Notes.*

The Art of Living was written on napkins in planes, restaurants, meeting rooms, and seminars all over this nation. Suddenly I would feel compelled to write an "aha" or insight I experienced. Each time I would notice the simplicity and the beauty of the Truth.

Finally, the Truth all seemed so simple. That's what the great philosophers and psychologists had been talking about for years. That's what Maslow's "self-actualized," Rogers' "fully-functioning," and Berne's "winners" were all about'! That's what Christ, Buddha, and Lao Tzu meant!

Whenever I would find myself being the "effect" of my experience and living out the Drama, I would reluctantly acknowledge that I was the cause. Once upon a napkin, I wrote:

> The Truth Is.
> > You can't escape it.
> > > Not because it's so good,
> > > But because the Truth communicates.
> > > Totally.

> There you'll be forgetting that you're
> > > > > > the Cause
> > (or conveniently negating it),
> > when all of a sudden
> > the Truth will seem overwhelming.

Making life work is like rowing with the current of the river; creating life not to work is like rowing up stream. You might reach the same destination, but "Oh my God, the price you have to pay!"

It is my intention
> that these words will have meaning for you,
> and that they will assist
>> you in experiencing the truth about
>> yourself-
>>> your relationships-
>>> your job - and
>>> your life.

Many know the science of living...
> which includes the mechanics of how to succeed, how
> to make money, how to gain status,
>> and how to handle the day-to-day functions.

Yet few
> seem to be aware of
>> the Art of Living,
> which is the ability
>> to experience the essence
>>> of what life has to offer,
>> to experience the melody, not just
>>> hear the music,
>> and to live your life artfully.

My love and support
> in your journey,

Gary Michael Durst

SEARCHING FOR
THE TRUTH

Once
A Truthseeker
Became frustrated. It seemed that
        No matter what
                Discipline he studied,
                Course he took,
                Religion he followed, or
                Book he read,

He just couldn't find
        The Truth.

So he decided to take a trip
        To a place where lots of people
        Are reported to know the Truth:
                                India.

When he arrived,
                The Seeker looked for a Guru.
                (Gurus are people who know what the Truth
                is.)
                He asked everyone
                The name of India's Top-Banana Guru.

After weeks of searching
The seeker came upon an Ashram.
(An Ashram is where Gurus hang out.)
The large sign in front said:
"The Guru is in, please take a number."

The Truthseeker was led to a room where he waited.
Finally, the Guru appeared.
He was a little guy with a big smile on his face.
(You always smile
When you know what the Truth is.)

"How can I serve you?", asked the Guru.
"Master, I have traveled a great distance.
I've tried so many ways to find the Truth.
Do you know what the Truth is?"

"Of course, I know what the Truth is.
How could I be a Guru
If I didn't know the Truth?"

"Sorry," said the Seeker, a bit embarrassed.
"Would you share the Truth with me?"

The Guru looked at the Seeker intently.
"It's just not that easy. Living is an Art.
To know the Truth,
You'll have to pay the price."

The Seeker gulped.
Of course there would be a price.
You don't get something for nothing!
A Guru would have to be out of his mind
To give the Truth away for free.

The Seeker, gathering courage, asked:
"How much money will it take?"
The Guru laughed.
"The Truth doesn't cost money.
The price is that you'll have to perform a service for ten years.
The task you are to perform is obvious."

The Seeker, who had been a disciple and a follower before,
Knew the story.
"I'll do whatever is necessary, Master."

"Good," said the Guru as he pointed.
"Do you see those barns down there?"

Indeed, the Seeker could not only see the barns,
He could *smell* the barns.

"Those barns are the dwelling place of the Sacred Cows.
In order for you to know the Truth,
You'll have to keep those barns spotless for ten years.
When you have performed the task,
Come back and I'll share
                              the Truth
                              with you."

The Seeker thought about what the Guru had said.
"Ten years...Ten years!!!"
There was no way he wanted to shovel
Cow dung for ten years, sacred or not!
No way!
But as he pondered, it became obvious by the way the Guru
Smiled
That the Guru knew something
That he didn't know.

If he could just figure out
The Truth
His life would work. Like the Guru
He could have that same Satisfaction and
                              Inner Peace,

And that would be worth any price.

"O.K., I'll do it!" The Seeker shouted triumphantly.

He began his task.
Days became weeks, weeks became months, months became
years.
The Seeker at times seemed like a robot.
He even forgot for long periods why he was shoveling.
He seemed to be doing it
Just to be doing it.

Finally, the last day came.

At sunset, he ran up the hill
To the Ashram
Where he had stood ten years earlier.

The Guru looked as though he had been
Expecting him.

Out of breath and stumbling
The Truthseeker shouted,
"Master, I've done it.
I've done it.
I've cleaned the dwelling place of the Sacred Cows for ten years.
Now, will you tell me the Truth?"

The Guru smiled.
"Yes, my son.
You've worked hard and you've kept your word.
Now you can know the Truth;
        The Truth is YOU ARE."

The Seeker said,
    "Yes, go on. I'm ready."

The Guru looked at the Seeker
and simply stated:
"That's it. That's the only Truth there is.
The Truth is YOU ARE.
You've spent your life asking that question and the last ten
Years discovering the answer."

Realizing that that was the extent of the message,
The Seeker stopped.
        The combination of
                anger,
                        fear,
                                humiliation,
                                        and disappointment
                Showed in his voice.

"I don't get it!
I shoveled and shoveled for ten years to find out: I AM!
I just don't get it."

The Guru just smiled and asked,

"How much more

            are you going to have to shovel
                Before you do get it?"

I. ABOUT BEING CONSCIOUS

The Truth is, "You Are."
It's been around
for thousands of years,
Great philosophers,
        religious leaders,
                sages and
                        prophets
                                have told us.

They've all told us,
                        and we've refused to listen.

The only
Truth in the universe
is "You Are."

That's it.

Few   want to accept the answer.

Few   want to see it that way.

Most of us want to hold on to our illusions
        that someone else knows the real Truth;
                or
        that we have to study for years to find it;
                or
        that only the wisest can know the Truth;
                or
        that only the wisest even care.

The Truth is
        Your Experience is your Reality.
        Your Reality is your Experience.

Your experience of the universe
        flows through you.
No one else
        is experiencing what you're experiencing,
        or what you have experienced,
        or what you will experience.

From where you're sitting right now,
there is only one truth
in the universe
and that truth comes
when you say,
        "I am."
That's all you can say,
because that's all you know,
and that's all you'll ever know.

(You *are* totally certain that you EXIST, aren't you?)

Of course. "These truths we hold to be self-evident."

But you're not so certain
        that anyone else really exists,
        or anything else for that matter.

(Maybe there's no one else out there.
Maybe life is just a damn good movie.)

We go on thinking that the world exists independently
        and we're independent of "it" or "them."

If you think the world is "real" and independent
        from you, (the source),
ask yourself how you would prove
that "they" exist.

Once you've proved it--
            notice the person to whom
            you proved it.

The wake-world reality of
        sensory perceptions are
only your experience...
        They don't *prove* anything...
        Anymore than a rose proves anything...
            A rose just is.

Your sensory perceptions are simply your sensory perceptions.

Maybe
        you made up your sensory perceptions
like you made up the rest of
        your universe.

You don't know that this book is
        "really"
in your hands right now
All you know is that you're having
        a sensory perception
of it. It feels solid. You can touch it,
see it, smell it, even hear and taste it.

But maybe,
      it's just another prop
        in the movie
      You're creating, called "This is your life."

And a damn good movie it is!
You've been playing your role
      so well
you even had yourself convinced.

Marvelous performance! Bravo!

You've written such a convincing
      plot it even fooled
        you:
           The writer,
           the main character,
           the director,
           the set designer,
           the choreographer,
           the make-up artist,
           the stunt man,
           the camera man.

You're not only in the movie,
you're also experiencing it.

Your experience always comes back to you.
When you look beyond your act, to your essence,
all you know is that
      you are.
And there's no way to prove it.
And no need to,

           You are   I am
           because   because
           you are.   I am.

Nothing could even have taken place
           until
you said, "I am." How could you notice
that you had done something if you weren't
aware that
      you were?

"You" wouldn't have been there for it
      because
"You" wouldn't have existed.

To exist
is
to participate
with the Awareness
of self: I AM.

I AM
      therefore I think, not vice-versa,
      therefore I feel, not vice-versa,
      therefore I sense, not vice-versa.

To say
      "I KNOW I AM"
is redundant.

Beingness
just
makes the statement
I AM.

And it's only verifiable to
         you.
It's the best kept secret in the universe.
It's the first,
         last,
            and only provable statement in the universe
               to you.

And that's the only person to whom you could
prove
it,
 because
    The Truth
        is
    You Are.

II. ABOUT BEING WHERE YOU ARE BY CHOICE

Once
you know
you are,
then, you have to ask,
"So, where am I?"

YOU ARE...
      HERE.

The strange thing about being
"here"
is that it's very possible
to not be here.

You can be two places at once.

(While reading this
your mind may be wandering...
for example, you may be
thinking
about the fact
that your car needs to be taken
to the garage.)

Let's say the last time you had the car repaired,
you became angry
because you felt you had been overcharged.
Through your mind's recall mechanism
you could relive the entire experience.

To find out where "here" is,
imagine that a piece of the ceiling above your head
                fell
                        right
                              now,
        while you were mentally re-experiencing
        the scene in the garage.

        Where would you feel it?
        Where you are sitting right now,
                  or
        in the garage?

"Here" is defined by your physical presence.
"Here" is where your body is.
We know we're here, because this is where
it's all taking place.
When the ceiling falls
you get to have a lump on your head here
in this room – not where
your mind
was.

That's one of the problems
with being two places at once.

It's dangerous!

When your mind abandons your body,
it can put both in jeopardy.

BEING UNCONSCIOUS CAN BE DANGEROUS

You can get your piece
taken away very easily!
In Monopoly, your piece is a
top hat,
a scotty dog,
a car.

In life, your piece is
your body.
Take your piece away
and the game is over.

You lost your turn.

Even if you don't lose a turn,
your body can get pretty scarred.
That's what happens in a universe
that's filled with ceilings that fall.

Accidents happen because
"Nobody's Home," mentally.

Your mind goes on vacation
and leaves your body to babysit.
Sometimes you become
"Lost in Space," and
that's when it's dangerous.

Ever get into your car and drive to your destination
and not be able to remember
driving there?
You don't remember, because your mind was "Out To Lunch."

That's usually when you get traffic tickets.
The cop is like a cosmic custodian
reminding you to stay conscious
when you drive.

You can't remember the drive because
you weren't there for it.
If you're not "here"
for the experience of life
you can do disastrous things
to yourself and others.

What's worse
is that when danger does occur
your mind always seems to want to "leave the scene"
                                    of the accident.

You enter an unconscious state,
which even further immobilizes you.
You become like an ostrich –
the mascot of unconsciousness.
Whenever an ostrich is frightened or bored,
it puts its head in one place
and its body in another.
It likes to stick its head in the sand,
where it's warm and comfortable.

Notice when you stick your head in the sand,
you put yourself in the ultimate vulnerable position.

(That's your ass hangin' out there in the breeze!)
And you keep wondering why you're getting kicked?

People, circumstances, and events keep shouting -
"Wake up, wake up, wake up!"

It's dangerous when your mind splits.
And that's just one of the problems...

When you're unconscious,
communication with another being is difficult,
if not impossible.

When you think about the times you had difficulty
communicating with others---
when they just didn't seem to "hear" what you had to say
or
when you didn't hear what they had to say---
       it was because one or both of you were unconscious...
         Your minds were somewhere else.

Maybe you were thinking about something else
or
rehearsing what you were going to say
or
the person said something that triggered an association,
and vice versa.

That's why most conversations are
      a one-way
communication, rather than a
      two-way
        sharing process.

Ever had a spouse or friend or boss
report that they gave you an important bit of information--

such as: Going to Jim and Sue's place for cocktails,
          Making certain that the letter went out on time,
          or
          Not to forget to pick up something from the store,
              and you didn't remember?
          (Of course.
          You probably weren't there for the communication.)

Besides being dangerous
        and creating a real communication problem,
        being "Unc", (unconscious), can make producing
                                results
                            very
                                time-
                                consuming.

A lot of people are paid for eight hours
        of work --
        for which
they're "there" for about two.
        (and that's usually lunch and breaks!)
Ever read the same paragraph fourteen times?
Spent two hours writing a short memo?
Taken a forty minute shower?
Washed a few dishes for what seemed to be hours?
It's difficult to perform a task when you're really not
            there for it.

You can miss a lot if you're not there for it.
Strangely, life continues,
        Experiences pass us by.
        You bought the ticket,
            but didn't get on the bus.

        LIFE is a "Be There For It" proposition.

        You might find less danger
            fewer accidents,
            deeper communications,
            more results
            and
            greater satisfaction
        if you decide to participate
            in your own life.

Participation does not mean
        analyzing
            or
        projecting.

It means experiencing what's there consciously right Now.

III. ABOUT LIVING <u>NOW</u>

The eternal instant is
                    Now.

        The only time
        you can be
            HERE
              is
            NOW.

Now is all there is.
        It
doesn't last any time
        at all
      It just is.
It exists outside of something called
        time.

Time is just a
        convenient recording mechanism.
Your mind has several filing systems.
Chronological order is one of them.

That's all for the mind's Records Department.
        It has nothing to do with what's happening.
You have never experienced anything, except
        NOW.

Your mind records the event and categorizes it, sequencing it
        into seconds, minutes, hours, weeks, months, and years.
        It generally conceptualizes it all as
        Past
        Present
        Future.

It looks like this:

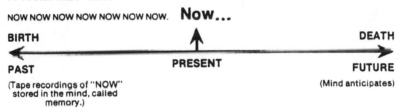

Usually we think of NOW as the present
        and that's true.
It's also true that NOW was the past
        and will be the future.

Look at it:
        When you were two years old, what time was it?
                NOW!
        And when you were sixteen, what time was it?
                NOW!
        And when you were twenty-two, what time was it?
                NOW!
It's always been right
                NOW!

And

when tomorrow comes, what time will it be?
NOW!

The future can only *exist* in now,
and the instant it does, it's not
future. Future is simply a mind
projection.

Now is all you have.

It's all you've ever had.
And it's all you ever will have.

Get the joke:
When is the time to clean up your life?
When is the time to make your relationship
work?
When is the time to produce results?
When is the time to stop lying to yourself?
When is the time to make those changes?
When is the time to start that project?

There is only NOW.
In that NOW you can produce a result,
tangible or intangible,
You have the choice:
You can either produce a result
or
you can prevent a result from
being produced.

A result can be produced when your mind
and your body are united.
When your mind is not functioning with your body,
it may be impossible to produce a result.

Not that your past memories aren't
useful
In producing results. They are.
In fact, those memory tapes are necessary for
survival.

You don't have to be constantly hit by cars
or burn your hand on stoves to notice it hurts.
  You can recall the memory tape of the original incident
  and learn from it.

  We learn physically, from our past tapes. Yet we
  neglect the same process that constantly saves our lives.

We should look at our past tapes as incidents
      from which we need to learn.

In other words, we need to ask what lesson is to be learned,
from that divorce, illness, accident or firing
rather than spending all of our time
justifying,
      bitching,
            blaming,
                  and being right
                        about the past event.

It's like constantly burning your hand on a stove,
      and bitching because it shouldn't be there.
Maybe, someday, you'll learn not to put your hand
      on top of the burner.

When you don't like the event,
      look at it and learn from it.
When you like the event,
      recall what was occurring and repeat it.

The mind can be
      the master
            or
      the servant.
It can search to shift cause and moan
            or
it can assist you along your journey.

The mind is the series of recordings
      actual, imagined, exaggerated, erased,
      or created, by the mind itself.
It's a never-ending cycle.
It not only records past events, it also projects future events.

The future doesn't exist. The past doesn't exist.
Only NOW exists.

You are indeed eternal.
What does your experience of past tell you?
How far back can you go?
Can you recall a time when you weren't?
Can you accurately remember when you didn't exist?

Your experience is that you've always existed.
You can't remember someone saying:

"Lights,
Film,
Camera,
OK, roll 'em.
Start the show."

From where you are right now, you don't know whether
your parents created you
or
you created your parents.
Notice how funny it is to bitch about what your
parents did to you!

And from where you sit, you can't think
of what it would be like not
to exist.
You'll never know.

What matters is that there is only one
time in which you can exist.
That one time is
NOW.
You may decide to use your mind
to learn from the past and to plan for the future
or
to bitch about the past and to worry about the future.

It's up to you. It's your life or non-life.
        Got any choice?
        The truth is you already chose.
You're here aren't you? You are reading this aren't you?

To BE, HERE, NOW is to be conscious.
To be conscious is to have your mind and body
        united in the same time-space frame.

To become Consciously Conscious-
                to be more alive,
                        to live life artfully,-
        may be a difficult game to play.

What you may have to do is confront that which
        you don't want to confront.

Consciousness is not a game that you
        "should"
        "ought"
           or
        "must"
play. You already are. It's a game you might
choose to play to increase your satisfaction.

You are the only one
        who can determine your own
                satisfaction.
This book, your loved ones, friends, therapy or seminars
        won't do it for you.
You're going to play or not as *you* see fit.
        when *you* see fit.
That's the way it works.

It's your choice to Be Here Now
or not.

The Truth is You Are.
So why not be Here for the experience of what's happening Now?

Why not experience
                your life,
        rather than
                simply going through the motions or the process?

IV. ABOUT EXPERIENCING YOUR ALIVENESS

Who Are You Really, and
How Did You Get To Be That Way?

In order to get in touch with who you are
        really,
we have to acknowledge how you became that
way in the first place.

It
all began
with Creation.

Once upon a moment of NOW
        you were
        conceived.
(Hopefully it was fun for someone!)

There you were,
        something
                from
                        nothing.

Being and changing.
Totally supported by the world's greatest life support system:
        Mother.

No light.
Temperature accurately controlled at 98.6 degrees.

The life-support tube:
      carried oxygen and disposed of poisonous gas,
          (no breathing
          no coughing
          no gasping for air)
      supplied food that was already digested,
          (no eating
          no hunger
          no acid-indigestion)
      carried away food wastes,
          (no elimination
          no constipation
          no diarrhea).

And you were weightless,
      comfortably floating in your own little
        heated pool,
No need to exert yourself. No where to go.

You started your taping sessions...
      Recording it all.
          No considerations,
             evaluations,
               fears, guilts, embarrassment, worry.
        Just direct and straight recording.

Gradually, you began to feel a bit crowded.
      You were out-growing your space.
      "If one more person moves into this neighborhood..."

One day, after about nine months,
The walls started to press in on you,
      then they stopped.
Mom started to get a bit upset.
      Her heart was beating
          faster and faster.
      She seemed to be gasping for air.
You felt your heart pounding,
      "Hey, what's happening?"

Then *WHOOSH!*

"Wait a minute, who pulled the plug?
Who's draining my swimming pool?"

The walls started squeezing you
        tighter and tighter
        faster and faster.

All of a sudden you felt real whoozy,
        so dizzy.
You could hardly stay there for the experience.

You could feel your head being squeezed
        through a small tunnel:

"It's too small.
I'll never fit. No way. My head's too..."

The ultimate pain subsided with a clear slide into

              LIGHT!!!
        "Oh, my God! It hurts... It's too bright!"

And it was so
              COLD!!!
It had always been 98.6 degrees.
Now you were freezing your ol' wazoo off!

And then there was all that noise. The talking.
        The clinking of instruments.

Someone's finger probed your mouth,
and drops were added to your eyes.
Finally you were picked up by the heels and
              SLAP!
Welcome to the Western World!

You began to shake from your own sound
and your own fear.

"Oh God, this is awful. Lord forgive them,
        they know not what they do!"

And then: They cut the life-support tube.

Instant death!
Cut off from all of life's process.
No food, no waste removal, no oxygen.

NOW you were on your

OWN.

Now you had to start scratching for your very

SURVIVAL.

And that's birth:

The first time you learned *NOT*
to
BE HERE NOW.

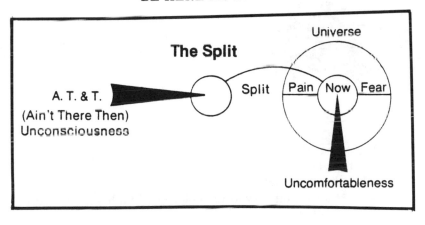

In order to survive the
fear,
pain,
and
suffering,
you created a mechanism that allowed you
a mental escape valve: AT&T

AIN'T THERE THEN.

Your mind split to
another time – space scene
where it was more comfortable

At that point you probably went back
                to your tapes of the womb,
                where the reality of survival needs
                didn't exist.

The same process continues now.
Your mind splits when you feel
                threatened or uncomfortable.
You go unconscious.

When threatened,
Your mind creates a place that doesn't exist -
                Never, Never Land.
                Fantasy Land.
Where there is no hostility or the
                uncomfortableness of the "real" world.

Splitting
        is
very functional
Deep within you -
        You knew at birth
                that if you stayed in such a painful, hostile universe
                too long
        you'd go crazy or die.

So, you chose the next best thing:

To go crazy in stages.

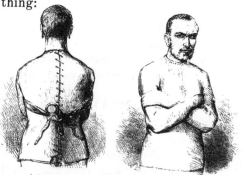

With each split, a new neurological path
     is formed.
     An association is made.
     Events become symbols
     and triggers for
more and more splits.

Eventually almost anything can trigger an escape
     into Fantasy Land.
At some point, you become more
     unconscious than conscious.

Your mind takes over:
     it dominates because
Survival is an important persuader.

In order to survive
your mind records everything
you've ever experienced.

It's like a computer that stores all the tapes using
an information retrieval system.

When you want information
your mind looks through the tapes
     to pull out the appropriate data.

The purpose of the stored information is
     to provide the knowledge of "How to Survive."

The storage contains
     memories, concepts, beliefs, and associations.

Paradoxically, even though the purpose of the tapes
     is survival,
     some of the responses and associations
     are so inappropriate
     that the body is put in jeopardy.

The cosmic Joke
     is that the mind
     is so intent on survival
     that it will sacrifice
        the body
     to insure that the tapes will survive.

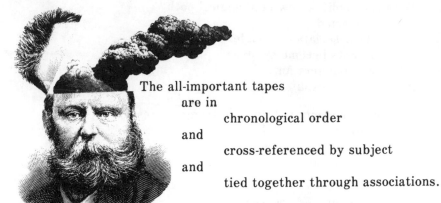

The all-important tapes
are in
      chronological order
and
      cross-referenced by subject
and
      tied together through associations.

Graphically, your mind would look like this:

The Mind

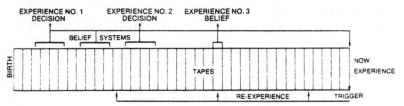

Anytime your mind desires
it can split from
    NOW,
go into the past,
and play any old tape.

And since the trauma of birth
    you've let your mind split whenever it chose.
It's as though you said to your mind:
    "OK' you saved my life, now you can split anytime you
    choose."

There's only one flaw:
               Your mind is often
               an absolute idiot!
Sometimes it pulls inappropriate data.
Sometimes the past response is not
    appropriate for the experience NOW.
Sometimes the mind gets stuck in a particular
    response and wants
        to play it over and over.

Eventually there are a lot of recurring themes:
  Look at the times you're angry;
    at the times you're frustrated;
    at the times you're embarrassed;
    at the times you're hurt;
  Notice the patterns and
    the triggers.

Don't you always have the same
    fight with your spouse?
When was the last time you said,
"Hey, honey, let's fight about
    something new tonight!"

Not too original in our behavior patterns, are we?

These automatic patterns begin to act as barriers:
  Barriers
          keeping us from experiencing
          the world,
and the world from experiencing us.

The walls we built to
          keep others out.
are also
          keeping us in.

The strongest automatic patterns are those
        related to our primal needs.
If we don't satisfy these needs, we die.
Primal patterns provide almost
        instinctive behavior to insure our survival.

The next level of automatic patterns
        are triggered by a set of symbolic needs.
A symbol
        is a representation that
        stands for something it isn't.

$ is a symbol for money.
It is not actually money. It won't buy you a cup of coffee.

You cannot satisfy your needs, psychologically, through symbols.
        You may think of possessions as symbols of security,
        and yet you may have all the possessions in the world
        and not have security.

Some of us use
        food
As a symbol of love. ("Good kids finish everything on their
plate.")
As a symbol for the elimination of physical pain.
                ("Oh, you fell down. Come inside, I'll give you
                a cookie.")
As a symbol for the elimination of psychological pain.
                ("Those kids won't play with me!"
                "Well, we'll just have an ice cream cone then.")

Symbolic behavior can be a little crazy:
        When you're happy, celebrating, and feeling loved
                you eat.
        When you're sad because you look unattractive and feel
        rejected
                you eat.
        When you feel guilty for having eaten too much
                you eat.

That's how much of an idiot your mind can be.
And how ridiculous patterned behavior can become.

BEING BOUND TO YOUR PAST

The more automatic responses you have
    the more your vision is restricted
    and you can't see what's really going on.

Since all that's necessary for an automatic reaction
    is a stimulus
life becomes a knee jerk reaction -
    a mental reflex.

Even events that are similar will run
    an old tape, evoking the same archaic feelings:

        Your boss gives you constructive criticism
        and you respond defensively,
        just like you did with your father years ago.

        Your spouse forgets to call,
        and you feel, "No one really loves me,"
        just like you did when you were a child.

When you ask someone who is programmed who they are,
they will tell you what they did yesterday.

We become robots,
        machines,
        computers.

Stimulus ⟷ Response   Stimulus ⟷ Response
Stimulus ⟷ Response   Stimulus ⟷ Response
Stimulus ⟷ Response   Stimulus ⟷ Response

The Wurlitzer

We become like Wurlitzers.
        A Wurlitzer
            is not a very happy person.

        Its records are stacks of tapes, recorded by the mind.
        You push the buttons
            for a replay of a particular tape
            to get the kind of "music" you want.

For example:
            Your spouse might push your A-11 button -
            "Why did you spend so much money?
            You know we can't afford it."

            You immediately bring out your tape to defend
                your position.

We become machines
        by running out our numbers,
            which become our automatic behavior patterns.

        The Wurlitzer
            seeks to develop programs to
                defend itself from every possible contingency.
            In order for it to work
                it has to be "plugged in."

This is a pretty grim view of humanity.
Being Machines. It can become depressing.
        There is very little aliveness.
And yet, you can't step outside of this reality
        anymore than
you can step outside of yourself.

We push each other's buttons, without even trying.
Notice how easily we plug into anger, upset, and hurt.
Once you slip into Out of Control,
                you've really gone unconscious.

Because of our button-pushing expertise,
the name of the game in most relationships is
        "I'll push yours - You push mine."

Being a Wurlitzer is bad news.

The good news is once you admit
        how mechanical and how programmed
                you are.
then you can start to live
        more the essence
        of who you really are.
        You can be more alive.

THE GOOD NEWS

Unlike the Wurlitzer, you can reach down
        and unplug the device.
You can defuse your own mechanical responses.

Of course, you may have to shovel some more smelly stuff
        before you comprehend that you're the cause
        of what's going on
        and
        before life starts to work for you.

And that's totally OK,
        because at least
                now you know
                        and
                now you know that you know.

Remember -
> Life seldom works out for people who
> don't know what's going on.

Automatic behavior patterns often act as barriers -
> Barriers that need to be transcended.

Yet when you're right up against a barrier,
life can become real uncomfortable.

Often the more uncomfortable it feels, the closer you
> are to a solution.

THAT WHICH YOU FEAR
CONFRONTING THE MOST
SHOULD BE WHAT YOU CONFRONT FIRST!

That's the area of your life that is taking away
most of your aliveness right now.

The instant you push beyond the barrier,
you'll notice that whatever you were afraid of
        vanished,
        evaporated,
        went poof!
just like that!

One of the problems, however,
        is that your mind always thinks
        it's silly,
                or it's too much work,
                        or it's too inconvenient,
                                or it's not appropriate right now,
                                        or it's too complicated,
                to make life work for you.

When you're up against a barrier, clarity is
        right there on the other side.
        That's what comes next.
The light at the end of the tunnel is there –
        you just have to open your eyes.

When you confront a barrier, you'll realize that it was
            a phantom.
        It was a product of your own imagination.

It will disappear in a cloud of smoke,
        and you'll ask yourself,
        "Why was I afraid of that?"

What good does it do you to fear something,
        except as a signal that you'd better take action now?

Fear can take away your aliveness right now.
It can take many forms:

        Embarrassment
            is the fear of exposure and
            of having people find out that you are
            actually the person you always feared you were.

        Anger
            is based on the fear that you might be wrong,
            or that you might not be listened to,
            or that people won't give you respect,
            or it may just be a fear that you're not all right
                the way you are.

        Hurt
            is a fear that someone doesn't love you,
            or appreciate you,
            or that they may share the same low opinion of you
                that you hold of yourself.

In order to break some of your automatic behavior patterns,
You may have to face your fears.

V. ABOUT CONFRONTING YOURSELF

Life is a
        series of problem-solving exercises.
Since you can always add new tapes,
it may seem like a never-ending,
        boring game.
The person who is totally in his tapes
        doesn't see any way out.

The way out
        is to play
                exactly the same way,
but to notice that there's a possibility
        that you are alive while doing so.
        To do that, dissipate some of your
        automatic behavior patterns.

Take a look at one of your problems right now.
        1. WHAT ARE THE TRIGGERS?
        2. WHAT DO YOU GET OUT OF HAVING IT BE THAT
            WAY?
        3. WHAT'S THE PATTERN?
        4. WHO GETS TO BE RIGHT?
        5. TELL THE TRUTH ABOUT IT ALL
                    and
        6. KISS IT GOOD-BYE.

What you'll experience is a rush of energy,
                        a new lease on life,
                        more spontaneity,
                        and another increment of
                        aliveness.

To rid yourself of a problem –
Stop looking at it as a problem. It's an
              opportunity
to be alive.

You have to stop making
        it wrong
        to have problems.

The only people without problems
          are those who are
                        six
                        feet
                        under.
          (And we're not too sure about them.
          They're just harder to interview.)

To be more alive
  you need to face
    your problems.

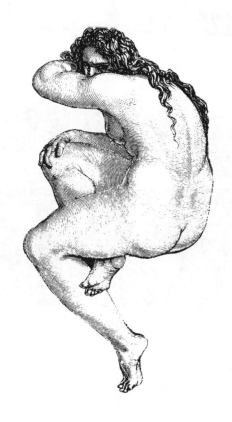

Remember:
    Whatever you're afraid to face
      will always
          bite you in the Ass.

1. What Are The Triggers?

You'll only be able to play
    "Locate the Trigger"
    when you're conscious.
You can't do it when you're in the middle of a taped response.

You have to wait until you're back in
    Here and Now.
After you've run your number –
    thrown your tantrum,
    pitched your bitch,
    had the same old fight,
    plugged into your boss –
        then you can ask
            "What was happening just before I
            went unconscious?"

Your triggers
    are what you need to examine.

In many cases, the original experiences
have been associated with so many
other
symbols,
that it all becomes
non-
sense.

As you know,
Many people would rather save their
        Cadillac
        than their own
        Ass.

The triggers may have become
      so symbolic
that whenever anyone even mentions
      money,
      sex,
      politics,
      or
      gets the least bit close to you –

                              you go unconscious.

A funny thing happens
      when you become conscious
      of the trigger:
You begin to dissipate some of
      the energy,
the moment you look at it.

The more
      energy you release from that tape.
the more
      freedom you will feel, and
the more
      "you"
      you will experience.

It takes a lot of time and energy to build and to maintain
      negative self-defeating responses.
And these responses keep you from
      experiencing
who you are and who you can become.

The negative energy that is on the tape
      makes your mind want to flee the scene
      whenever it gets close to anything remotely associated.

Yet putting your hand over your eyes
      doesn't make the world go away.
You're still experiencing your experience
      whether you want to look at it or not.

When you begin to examine triggers
      that start automatic behavior patterns,
initially you may think--
      "It doesn't work"
because you're still experiencing the same old Drama.

At first,
    you may only
    shorten the cycle
    by maybe a minute or even a second.
The second time
    you look at the trigger,
    the automatic tape may be a little bit
    shorter.

Sometimes you will be unable to detect the difference
    until
    all of a sudden, you say -

"God, something like that used to get me so plugged in
    and upset
and this time I hardly even noticed it!"

"YOU SPENT <u>HOW MUCH</u> ON THAT DRESS?!!"

If you simply care enough about
        yourself
and the people you love,
        to persist
in confronting those negative taped responses,
        you'll start seeing,
                        and feeling,
                the results.
                                And so will they.

You won't go out "there"
        quite so far
                or
        stay quite so long.
You'll experience less unconsciousness.

When you first start to
        dissipate the energy--
        bound to the past
        and
        start to use it
        Now,
        you may start to feel
        High.

That's how it feels
        to confront something really difficult
        and win.

It's a good feeling to know that
        you'll again have all the energy
        that was tied up in the tape.

You can use it
        however you choose:
                to mend thyself,
                to be more productive,
                to be more loving,
                to become conscious of your own life.

Locate the trigger
        so you can notice the tape,
                so you can confront the issue, and
                        so you can experience more aliveness.

2. What Do You Get Out Of Having It Be That Way?

The second part of the game--
    after you've played,
    "Locate the Trigger,"
        is
    "Determine the Payoff."

The tapes
    and the automatic behavior
                responses
exist to serve a purpose.

Your payoff may be
    to defend yourself against fear,
    to make someone else wrong,
    to protect your incredible ego,
    to have something to bitch about.

To determine your payoff
    you have to look at what
    you get out of having the
        situation that way.

Your problems
    may be your abilities.

For example:
    Your problems with _____

            may be your ability to get people
            to feel sorry for you.

YOUR PROBLEMS MAY BE YOUR ABILITY TO GET OTHER TO FEEL SORRY FOR YOU

Having a lousy relationship at least gives you
        something to talk about--
        just no satisfaction.

You're the only one
        who knows the payoff
        for you.
Asking someone else what *you*
        get out of the situation
is like asking someone else
        to have an orgasm for you.

Locate the trigger and tell the truth about it.
Face what you get out of having it be that way.

3. What Are the Patterns Involved?

When you determine your payoff,
  you'll notice recurring themes...

For instance.
    If you always had incompetent bosses,
        Maybe your payoff was that you were able
            to make them wrong.
        (*They* were always the sons-of-bitches!)
        Maybe you were able to tell others
            what a rotten boss you had.
        Maybe you were able to make your boss
            responsible for your mediocre performance.
        Maybe you were able to re-experience
            the same familiar themes you had with your
                                                    parents.

Or
      If your spouse always spent too much money,
            Maybe your payoff was that
                  you got to be right about the need for money.
            Maybe you were able to feel like the only responsible
                  party.
            Maybe you were able to play some old tapes
                  that you heard at home
                  when you were raised.

What you're beginning to realize is how many
      patterns you have.
      Some take a few minutes
      Some take a few weeks.
      Some take relationships to fulfill.
      Some take a lifetime.

Perhaps the same things that cause you problems on your
                                          current job
      are the same things that caused you problems on your
                                          last job,
            and the one before that,
                  and the one before that,
                        and the one before that.
Perhaps
      what's causing problems in this marriage
      may be the same factors that caused problems
      in your last marriage.

Until you're willing to face it,
      the old theme will always be there.

Determine the patterns
                  so you can end the cycle.

4.   Who Gets To Be Right?

You created the patterns
      to get
      something out of them
and now you need
      to tell the truth about that, too.

Many of us set up
      automatic behavior responses
      to get out of
      responsibility.

As long as you can make
      your boss
      your spouse
      your secretary
      your kids
         or
      your parents

      -wrong-

You don't have to take
responsibility
for
results
or
the lack of results.

If you persist in looking
      at your payoff, honestly,
      to see what you get out of having
      it be that way --
it always seems to have something to do with
      getting out of your own
         fundamental responsibility
         in that matter.

You get to be right...
      and alone.

5. Tell The Truth About It All

Stop lying about who created your
    problems.

To guarantee that you get stuck
    on a problem,
    blame someone else for it.

When you stop putting energy
    into
    blaming
    other people, circumstance,
        and events for what's
        going on in your life.
you're on your way.

You created your own tapes
    and automatic responses.
You're holding them in place
    with your own energy.

Whatever the problem is--
    if you keep running from it,
    if you keep turning your back on it,
    if you keep going faster to avoid it,
        it'll still be right behind you.

You become
    like a dog
    chasing its own tail --
Wake up to the fact -- that it's all you.

When you begin to tell the truth
    about your taped responses--
when you've paid your dues,
when you've shoveled enough shit,
    then you'll notice a geometric
        progression
                into
                    awareness.

The mechanism of an automatic behavior response
        cannot stand the focus
        of your consciousness
and cannot maintain itself when
        you take responsibility for it.

A demolition expert
        knows where to put the charges
        to blow the building sky-high.

You

        must demolish your taped responses
        and only
        you know where to put the
        dynamite.

After you've blown up the automatic response
you may hear echoes or reverberations.
        A trigger will hit you
        and you'll go
            -zip-
        in and out
                and
        back again.

You'll start to realize that the
automatic behavior mechanism
        is faulty.
It just won't run all the way out there
        like it used to.
You'll just say, "Oh, yeah, good ol' number E-7,
        I remember that one!"

Your old numbers will sound
        as empty as echoes.
You'll sit and stare at that
        which had always triggered you into unconsciousness
and it won't work anymore.

                    You'll just start to let things
                        be the way they are
                            and that's
                                when life begins to flow.

SUMMARY

Of course, you can still plug in
  whenever you want.
All you have to say is
  "I'm not responsible."
Your old number will come up
and you'll be able to run it out as
  long as you want.

But then,
That's what got you into this mess
  in the first place.
The good news
  is that you don't have to be on "automatic pilot,"
    you don't have to be a Wurlitzer,
    you can do something about it.

  You're the only one who can.

And
  I already know
    that
  you already know
    everything
  that I know
    and that you've been avoiding
      acknowledging it.

Because
  that would mean
  that you've **been** responsible for your past experience,
  that you **are** responsible for what you're
    experiencing now,
  that you **will be** responsible for your
    experience in the future.

To avoid taking the responsibility
you've been playing dumb.

(Now that's really dumb,
because the joke's on you.)

Avoidance doesn't change the truth
or the way it is.

With jokes like that,
here's hoping
you have a good sense of humor.

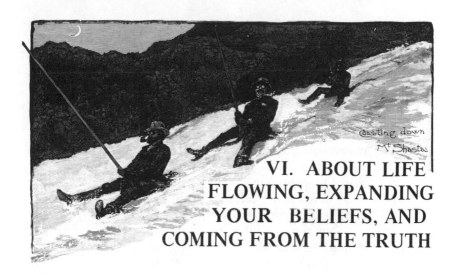

VI. ABOUT LIFE FLOWING, EXPANDING YOUR BELIEFS, AND COMING FROM THE TRUTH

I've Got Some Bad News,
And Some Good News!

The Bad News
        is that you're a Wurlitzer
        with tapes from the past,
        with automatic behavior responses,
        with buttons that can be pushed anytime.
        And the more automatic you are
        the less you know it and
        the less you're willing to admit.

The Good News is
        you're not just a Wurlitzer.
        You're also a tube!

A tube?

What does the most self-actualized,
        fully-functioning Guru
        do
        when he gets up in the morning?

(He empties his tube.
        just like you do.)

Isn't life exciting?
Every morning you get up and empty your tube.
Then you get dressed and fill your tube
        with breakfast.
Afterwards you grab a cigarette and stick it into your
        input hole.
Then you go to work
        drink some coffee--and fill your tube.
At break, you empty your tube
        so you can fill it up again.
At lunch--guess what?
        You fill your tube, then empty it
        before you go back to work.
At your afternoon break, you empty
        your tube and fill it.
Finally it's quitting time and you can
hardly wait to fill your tube at dinner.
After dinner, you watch TV and
        periodically fill and empty your tube.

Before you go to bed you empty your tube again
so the next day you can start
        the same
                exciting
                        process
                                all over again.
The only reason
        you have arms and legs is
        to get you from
        the refrigerator to the john!

If you wanted to eliminate the
        middle man--
        you'd put the refrigerator in the john!

Once you realize how much of your life is
        spent in
carrying out pre-programmed responses
        and in
filling and emptying your tube--
you have to ask--
        What am I doing here?"

What's the purpose?
Why are we experiencing life?

The age-old question.
The simple answer:

We are here experiencing life
so that we might
        experience life.

Not just the peaks,
        but also the valleys,
Not just the highs,
        but also the lows.

You're here
                to experience
                all
                of it.

And what do we all want out of our experience of life?

Satisfaction.

Out of each experience
in your life
what you really want is
satisfaction.

It's the bottom line.

You're not working for money,
you're working for the satisfaction
you hope that money can bring.
You're not in the relationship
for any other reason
than the satisfaction it can produce.

All there is in the universe is
experience.

You are an experience-tube.

You are a vehicle
through which the
experience of life passes.

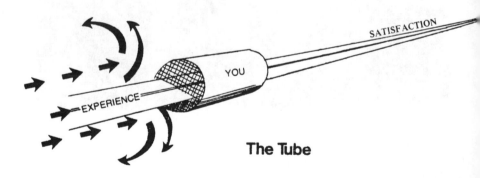

The Tube

The problem is
you've got a screen
in front of your tube that blocks out much of the
experience that life has to offer.
It keeps you from
a large part of you.
The screen
is made up of your beliefs about your reality.

The beliefs that restrict your
        view of reality are those
that you've made totally
        right,
        reasonable,
        logical,
        justified,
        and
        provable.

You look at all your potential
        experiences
and you make judgments
        about whether they are
                good
                or
                bad,
                        right
                        or
                        wrong,
                                moral
                                or
                                immoral,
                                        crazy
                                        or
                                        sane.

And somewhere in the back of your mind, is the truth:
        that they are, "None of the Above."
                They just are.

What takes place
        in front
                of your tube
                        is
        the Experience of Life.

The Experience
        either
        flows through the tube
                or
        it hits the screen
        and flows around you.
        (And you never know it.)

It's like being a
        wallflower
saying, "Look at all those people having fun!"
There you sit
        wishing, hoping or just wondering
                "What the hell is going on?"

WHY NOT COME TO THE PARTY?

When you don't allow the
        experience of life
                to flow
through you, you become a wallflower.
        It's happening
                all around you
and you've protected yourself
from that which you desperately
        need
to make life meaningful and satisfying.

The beliefs that keep you from experiencing
    are the same ones
    that shape the fabric of your universe.

They are a product
    of your education, your upbringing,
    your parents, your society.
Everything that has gone into making
    you
    be
    the you
    you are.

You've built this screen that tells you
    what kinds of experiences you can have,
    what's good and bad,
    what status you should achieve,
    what kind of
        job/house/spouse/car/children/neighborhood
            you should have,
    how much money you should make,
    who would make the "right" kinds of friends,
    who would make the right spouse.

And if anything
    doesn't fit your belief of how it should be,
    you
    just don't experience it.
        (That'll show it!)

Whatever you believe, you see as the truth
    And it either is, or it becomes that way for you.
Christ knew that and attempted to share
    it with the Apostles,
    but had a difficult time of it
    because they had not yet
    experienced it.
It's something you just can't tell anyone.

Your belief systems
    insulate you
    from
    everything that doesn't
    agree with them.

(They keep you from having the experience of nonagreement.)

Your belief systems
	will even use science
	(which is itself an organized system of beliefs
		about the universe)
	to prove the belief...and it does.
	(that is, until the agreement in the scientific world shifts.)

Every great scientist had to transcend
	the then current set of beliefs
and gain consensus from peers
	that his new set of beliefs was better.

Our egos are so large,
	our minds so strong,
		that even when we find an
		exception to our belief,
we use it to prove the rule, rather than disprove the rule.

For instance, prejudice is simply a series of
	particular beliefs focused
	negatively on a particular group.
	These aspects are considered to be inherent
	within each member of that group.

Let's say that you have a belief that
	men			relatives
	Mexicans		union members
	Blacks			school teachers
	Italians		executives
	Puerto Ricans		poor people
	women			rich people
	children		etc

								are "lazy."

Then you notice that the person down the street is a member
		of that group,
		but works
			his ol' wazoo off.
What your mind says is, "Sure, so and so works hard,
			but then he's the exception, because
			everyone knows that they're all lazy."

SOMETIMES THERE ARE BARRIERS TO CONFRONT

You may hold the belief
   that women make lousy managers
   because they're too emotional.
You'll say, "Jane is a great manager. She's not too emotional.
        But she's the exception. Because, as everyone knows
        women make lousy managers
            because they're too emotional."

Sound familiar?

You hold certain
        beliefs about reality
            which
        create your reality
            and then
        you smugly say,

        "I told you so."
            or
        "Sure 'Nough!"

YOU CREATE YOUR OWN REALITY.

Your beliefs
        totally manifest themselves
        and that has little to do with logic.
Your beliefs may be
        limiting
        the experience of what life has to offer.
Once you
        transcend
your beliefs
        you'll find yourself in a very different world.

Your belief systems about
    love often
limit the individuals with whom you can
    experience love.
Look at all the considerations you have about
    sex, age, body type, hair, eyes, lips, breasts, car,
    house, education, interest, voice, money, clothes,
    mouth, acne, etc., etc.
These considerations limit your sources for love,
    (much less sex.)

Life is not a discard.

It's an
    inclusive reality where
    the more you give
    the more you get.

Some of our basic beliefs
        don't have much basis, now.
The most potent ones come from early childhood
when you lived at home with the
        "giants" called "Mom" and "Dad"
        who did "magic" like prepare food, drive cars, and
        open doors, get you drinks of water,
        make you feel better when you were sick.
They were so powerful.
And you seemed clumsy,
                        weak, noisy, and bothersome.

Knowing that your very
        survival
        depended on them,
you made what they had to say
        "significant."
It was as though they had the
        power
to tell you what was going to happen to you
        forever.

However, some of what the Giants
        said was
                ridiculous,
                insane and
                inappropriate.

Perhaps you heard:
        "You're lazy"
        "You can't do anything right"
        "You'll never amount to anything"
        "Stupid"
        "You drive me crazy"
        "You're a clumsy ox"
        "You never finish anything on time"
        "You just can't be trusted"
        "You big cry baby"
        "You're too sensitive"
        "You never listen"

        ...and you believed it!!

71

This may be a shock to you
　　　　but...
you're not two years old anymore.
Your parents never had magical
　　　　powers to cause you to be anything you didn't *choose* to be.

You may not be that way at all.

All you have is
　　　　NOW.
You're the one
who decides
　　　　who you are and
　　　　what's right for you
　　　　NOW.

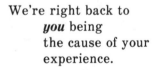

You can't even blame your
　　　　parents
and make them responsible.
That's a great game
　　　　and total b.s.

In large families parents can give
　　　　each child the same message.
Some accept it.
Some reject it.

We're right back to
　　　　you being
　　　　the cause of your
　　　　experience.

Your beliefs about who you are and
　　　　what you can become
are imposed limitations that you've made reasonable.

The only difference between you
　　　　　　　　　　　　　　and
　　　　　　　　　　　　　　the president of the company
is that the president has given himself or herself
　　　　　　　　permission to be "president"
　　　　　　　　　　　　　　and
　　　　　　　　　　　　　　you haven't.

Millionaires have transcended
their beliefs
that they couldn't be millionaires.
(Notice the results.)

Take a look at some of our
society's beliefs:
"Have fun, kid, because when you get into the cold, hard,
cruel world, it'll be no picnic."
"Live it up now, because when you get married, it'll be
different."
"Just wait until the kids come."
"If anything can go wrong, it will."
"You can't trust anybody."
"Give a person an inch and he'll take a mile."
"If you want something done right, you have to do it yourself."

We unconsciously follow
our beliefs and make them
right.
The girl who has a belief that
"Men are only after one thing..."
May be unconsciously flirting
with men, so that every time
One makes a pass at her, it proves
her mother was right.

73

Rightness
and
proof
can keep you stuck.

You selectively perceive what you want to perceive.
        Drive down a busy street:
        if you're hungry, you'll see restaurants.
        if you're thirsty, you'll see bars.
        if you're low on gas, you'll see gas stations.

When you change your perception of yourself,
        the people, circumstances, and events also change.

Wouldn't it be nice to take off your blinders and
        see what's really out there?
Wouldn't it be great to see yourself as the person
        you really are?

Many people are more afraid of
        success, rather than
        failure.
To be successful, would be to go against the
        beliefs
acquired earlier in childhood.
It's scary to be on stage, when you've
        just been handed
        a new script.
The old one may have been a real bum
        act:
but at least you knew your part
        and you knew
                how it was going to end.

No one ever told you that
if your life has become
                a soap opera,
                a melodrama
                        or
                a tragedy
that you can change it,
        or you can walk off the stage.

Someone told you that was the way it was;
and that was the way it had to stay.
You believed them
          and
you've been making them right ever since.

It's time to come from your own
experience, rather than your
beliefs or someone else's beliefs.

Complete the following:

I am —————— because ——————
                              ——————
                              ——————

I am _____ because ——————
                              ——————
                              ——————

I am _____ because _____
                              ——————
                              ——————

List all the "becauses."

The "becauses" are the beliefs
     standing in the way of change.
The word itself says it all:
     be cause: "Be" the "Cause."

Beliefs keep us
                    stuck
and they're the mechanism with which
     we keep others stuck
Often the belief systems have to do with what you
     can't do.
The word "can't" often means "won't."

Every time you say
     "I can't"
you justify why you aren't.

You don't have to defend
what's happening right now.
The universe is what
          it is.

Judgements and interpretations about the way it is,
    rob you of your experience of it.

It's your beliefs
        which act as a grid in
                front of your tube
limiting your experience.

Even though you have a screen, some of your
        life experience flows through your tube and
        you experience what life has to offer.
Other experiences, however,
        get stuck in your tube.
That which gets stuck are all the
        lies you've told.

You *know* what you can do and
        what your abilities are.
Everytime you say
        "I want that"
and you don't take responsibility
        to get it -
        it gets stuck in your tube.
All of your unrealized goals and
                unfinished projects
        get stuck in your tube.

The new car you said you wanted to have
        and you don't have it?
                        That's stuck in your tube.

The degree you said you wanted
        and don't have?
                        That's stuck in your tube.

The new living room set
        you don't have?
                        That's stuck in your tube.

That ten pounds you said you were going
        to lose, and haven't?
                        That's stuck in your tube.

That promotion you were in line for
        and you didn't get?
                        That's stuck in your tube.

Human Being Suffering
from Terrible Disease:
COSMIC CONSTIPATION!!

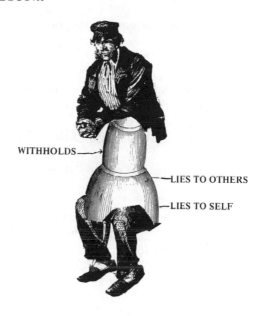

WITHHOLDS

—LIES TO OTHERS

—LIES TO SELF

Your tube gets clogged.
>You've become solid as a rock.
>Nothing can pass.
>>Everything you've said you wanted and don't have
>>>is stuck.
>>Everything you've said you wanted to stop and
>>haven't
>>>is stuck,
>>They are all lies you told to yourself.

Pretty soon you get
>Cosmic Constipation.

When you're constipated what do you
>think about all day?

You constantly re-experience
>your failures
because they often are manifestations of lies.

The blockage keeps you from being able to
    choose
    a new goal.
    The tube keeps getting more and more
                      constipated.
    Many people get to the point where they
                    give up.
They tire of all the strain.

Do you know anyone with Cosmic Constipation?
Take a look at the person who's
    sitting in the chair that
    you're sitting in right now.

    No wonder life doesn't flow.

    How could it?
You've become stuck in so many ways,
              in so many areas of your life,
you've begun to feel a bit
          sluggish.

These lies are not
           sins
    that will cause you to go to Hell when it's all over.
                  You won't have to wait.

When you lie, it is Hell.
You Unc out everytime.
Your lies drive you crazy.
You always pay yourself back for the
    lies you tell.

And the lies you tell yourself are the
    fundamental
    rip-offs -
Get the joke:
    "I think I'll lie to the only person who
    always knows the truth about my experience: Me!"

What do you think constant lying does to your gut?

If you're ill,
          sick,
                  depressed or otherwise
                    in pain -
clean out your tube - clean up your life
      and see how you feel.

Withholds are vicious
      because you always pay yourself back.
You don't have the same satisfaction with that person.
      Communications won't flow easily.
      You won't feel good.

A LIE IS A BURDEN WE CARRY
AROUND WITH US

You've got two
    and only two options
    in cleaning out your tube:

Number one: JUST DO IT.

    If you have unrealized goals stuck in your tube,
    you'll have to complete them, so your life will
    start to flow again.

Number two: TELL THE TRUTH ABOUT IT.

    You didn't want it anyway. Ain't that a bitch?
    Think of all the dues you had to pay to
    get it stuck in the first place! Look at all
    the rationalizations, reasonableness, excuses and
    rightness that you've used to justify not completing
    the action. To get your life to flow you'd have
    to give up all that b.s.   Pity.

Not only do the lies you tell yourself
    get stuck in your tube
    but so do the
lies you tell others.

Your lies to others are in two forms:
>Blatant Lies:
>>("Honey, sorry I have to work late tonight....")

and
>Withholds:
>>Manifestations of the truth recognized but not
>>communicated. ("What she doesn't know won't hurt
>>her.")

(Hell no - it won't hurt her - it'll kill you.)

Don't kid yourself:
>lies and withholds create a
>>physiological response.
>>>That's how a lie-detector test works.

Some of our most significant
>withholds are
>positive.
You don't share with your spouse/parents/ kids/friends/
co-workers
>how much you love them,
>how much you appreciate what they do,
>how much they mean to you.

What are you waiting for?
>a catastrophe?
>an illness?
>a quit?
>a divorce?
>their death?

Grief is often a function
        of the loved one dying with
        lies and withholds.
        "Oh, if I had only TOLD them how much I cared..."
Unless you get off an dramatic funeral scenes,
        why not do it
                NOW?

Your lies and withholds have
been keeping you from truly experiencing that other person.

If your relationship isn't working, it's because
        of the
                lies and withholds.
No technique, no therapy, no encounter week-end, no book
        will help
        until you've taken the responsibility of
        cleaning up your relationship.

Lies and withholds and satisfaction
        cannot occupy the same space.
Lies take away your aliveness,
                        your consciousness,
                        your satisfaction.
That's quite a price to pay.

The more lies within a company
        the less satisfaction for the employees who work there.
The more lies within a family
        the less love experienced.
The more lies within a classroom
        the less growth that takes place.

The more lies between us
        the less we communicate.

Your life works to the extent
        that you're
willing to tell the truth about how you
        set it up.

"The truth shall set you free."
(What do you think He was talking about?)

And you always
      know the truth
         about your lies.

You can't kid yourself
      because you always know the results.
You can always prove that
      you didn't want the goal you said you wanted.
If you don't have it - that's all
      the proof you need.

If there's no energy on the lie
      you don't have to mess with it anymore.
If there's still energy - if it's still bothering you -
      you'd better handle it.
You're the only one who knows, and
      you're the only one paying the bill.

It's like the expression from the Old West,
    "You've got to separate the horseshit from the gunsmoke."

The truth is:
    Life is satisfaction/love/results
        or the bullshit as to why it isn't.

It's D.D.S.
   Dog Doo Simple:
         You've either stepped in it or you haven't,
         and you know right away.

You either have satisfaction or lies.
You're either digging it or bitching about it.
You're either expanding or contracting.
      There ain't no middle ground,
      no grey - It's
      on or off.

There's no other place from whence
      to play.

To make life work
   to get more aliveness.
      to become more conscious,
         to make your relationship work...

Tell the truth about who gets to be right; about your payoffs,
      patterns, and decisions; about your automatic behavior
         responses.
Take 100% responsibility for your experience now.

Stop blaming other people, circumstances or events.

Start being who you are - a loving, ethical being
      dedicated to producing satisfaction for
         self and others.
Share with others so you can be around people who
      are alive, loving, and kind.

And then just
            sit back
                  and enjoy
                        the party.

Now that *is* the Good News!

VII. ABOUT GIVING UP THE DRAMA AND THE BAD FEELINGS

If It's My Party, Who Are These Other People?

If the
        only truth in the universe is
            "I AM"
then who are these other people in my experience?

You just can't be too sure.
        Maybe there's no one else out there!
        Maybe they're all just a part of your reality bubble.

What you see in others is simply your own reflection.
When you look at
        someone else
            you're looking into a mirror.

It's as though that
        great-cosmic-part of you
        didn't like playing alone
        so it went
        "poof"
        and created another part of you
            to play with,
and you lied about that, too.
You said the other was a "notself"
                            a "someone else"
                            a "not me"

You said the other
                had nothing-to-do-with-you.

Take a look in the mirror again.

"Mirror, mirror, on the wall,
        who is the who of us all?"

"I am."

All beings are a reflection of you.

And you are a reflection of all beings.

Love thy neighbor
as thy self.

Do unto others as
you would have
others do unto
you.

This is the sum of duty: Do
naught unto others which would
cause you pain if done to you.
Brahmanism - Mahabharata: 5, 1517

Hurt not others in ways that
you yourself would find hurtful.
Udana-Varga: 5, 18

Surely it is the maxim of loving-
kindness: Do not unto others that
you would not have them do unto
you.
Confucianism - Analects: 15, 23

No one of you is a believer until
he desires for his brother that
which he desires for himself.
Islam - Sunnah

What is hateful to you, do not to
your fellowmen. That is the entire
Law; all the rest is commentary.
Judaism - Talmud: Shabbat, 31a

Every religion promotes
"The Golden Rule"
because all religions have been
teaching aspects of the truth
or
they wouldn't have survived.

Notice the statement
        "Love thy enemies..."

Of course, you need to love your enemies as well as your
friends. They're also a part of you. Perhaps they're
that part that you fear,
            that you don't like about yourself,
            that you refuse to accept in you,
            that you don't want anyone to know about,
                    including yourself.

If you don't like
            what you see
            in others
        take a good hard look
            at yourself.

Mirrors don't lie.

When you start to accept yourself
        the way you are,
you'll allow others more freedom
        to be the way they are.

When you focus on aspects of yourself
        that you don't like,
you continually create those same aspects in others
        until they are resolved within you.

Once you're able to allow the other people
        to be who they are
and realize that you are the "cause"
        of your relationship with them,
        then you can stop
                bitching about the fact
                        that people are exactly the way they
                        are.

Then maybe you can start to
        communicate with them.

You are the cause in your relationships.
The strange thing is
we're all out to change the other guy:

Parents want to change their kids.
Kids want to change their parents.
Husbands want to change their wives and vice-versa.
Teachers want to change their students and vice-versa.
Bosses want to change their employees and vice-versa.
Public officials want to change people and vice-versa.

The *cause*
      is
         you.

Be the way you want your kids to be.
Act the way you want your spouse/teacher/boss/employee/
                 to act.

And stand back and watch what happens.

If you want to
        change
        someone else--
        start with you.
The other person's behavior is simply a reflection of your
    beliefs and behavior.

Aren't your kids terrible when you've had a bad day?
Don't your subordinates use the same excuses you give yourself?
Don't your customers give you your own objections?

Your experience
        of others
                is
        a result
                of
        your intention,
        conscious or unconscious.

When you like what you see in others,
        you acknowledge your reflection.
When you don't like what you see,
        you say, "That's not my intention!"

Really?
        Whose intention is it?
        Is God punishing you?
        Did the Devil make you do it?
        Are the Martians directing your actions?

Is someone sitting in your chair?
Is someone else paying your bill?

Notice that if you resolve the problem
        from your side
        there's no problem.

No solution requires two people.

Two people pushing
        against
                one another
create stress
        through resistance.
If one stops pushing
        there's only flow.

It takes two
                to tango
                to make war
                to argue.
It takes one
                to solve the problem
                to stop the aggression.

War
is a no-win/no-win situation.
Psychological games are
a no-win/no-win.
To play from "I lose/you win" - is a loss.
To play from "I win/you lose" - is a loss.

Why Lose?
Why do we set up "no-win" situations?
Why would we have negative experiences?
Why, if you're a reflection of me, do we have to go
through all this?

It's very simple:
to be Dramatic.

We continually lie
to ourselves and others
to make our lives dramatic.

The greatest lie
in the universe is
"I'm not responsible for my experience."
(Who put you there?)
(Who's going to have to get you out of it?)

When you play life from a position of
"no responsibility"
you can play a wonderful role called "The Victim."

Victims take no responsibility
by definition - that's what makes them Victims,

In order for there to be a Victim
there has to be a Persecutor.

If there's a Persecutor around
you can bet there's a Rescuer.

Steve Karpman says those three roles,
    Victim,
    Persecutor,
    Rescuer,
provide all the Drama in our lives.

The dramatic action comes from switching roles on the
    Drama Triangle:

The Drama Triangle

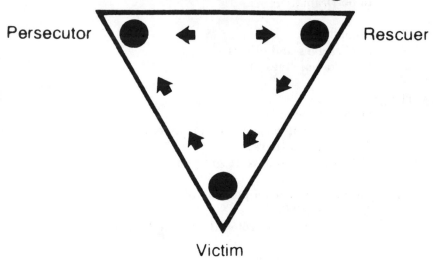

Persecutor   Rescuer

Victim

PERSECUTOR, RESCUER, VICTIM

The Classic Story

John Jones can hardly wait to get home from work
to tell his wife how much the boss has been
         persecuting him all day. Poor Victim.

Jane Jones can hardly wait till John comes home
so she can tell him how the kids have been
         persecuting her all day. Poor Victim.

The Jones kids are awaiting the arrival of their
father, John, because mother has been telling them
all day,
         "Just wait till the persecutor comes home.
         He'll punish you." Poor Victims.

Enter Victim John, greeted by Victim Jane, who
immediately reports her plight. Victim John turns
into Rescuer John, in order to help his damsel, and
yet feels victimized saying, "Aw Shit, now I've got
to play Persecutor, when I wanted to be Victim."

Angrily he stomps into the kid's room – and
"lets them have it."

Rescuer Jane hears their pleas, and enters just
in the nick of time to rescue the kids and to
persecute John for being so mean.

Victim John stomps out of the house and goes to the
bar, hoping to find someone to "understand" (rescue) him.

Tune in
    tomorrow, folks, for another
    exciting episode of
    "As the Stomach Turns".

Those three roles create
lots of Drama -
    just
        no Satisfaction.

Satisfaction only comes from the truth.
All three positions are based on lies:
    Victims always try to get out of their
        responsibility. They take 0% responsibility.
    Rescuers try to "help" victims by
        taking responsibility for them.
        That's 200% responsibility.
    Persecutors try to force the victim to do something
        and feel that if it weren't for
        them, nothing would happen.
        They also play it from a
        200% position.

Playing life from 0% responsibility or 200% responsibility
    is a lie.
We all have 100% responsibility for our experience.
There are no helpless Victims in the Universe.
Victims always want to convince you
        that they had no responsibility in the matter.

Let's say you're standing at a four-way intersection.
And you're about to be the star of Victim Productions.
You look
        and the light turns green and says,
            "Walk"

So you know you're doing the
        "right thing"
and you go unconscious, not noticing
    the bus
    that just ran the red light
    and
    flattens your piece in the middle of the
        intersection.

What good does it do for you to yell -
        "I had the right of way"
        "He ran the red light"
        "I'm the helpless victim"

Who has the flattened piece?
Who is dead right?
Who has to pay the bill for your experience?

Even if your piece
        isn't totally flattened -
if you just became a double amputee
        in a wheel chair -
what good would it do you to blame the
        bus driver for the rest of your life
        for what he did to you?

Notice your experience always comes back to you.
You're the one who
                        did everything necessary
                                        to produce the result.

That was *you* who chose to be in that city at that time,
        wasn't it?
That was *you* who chose to go down the street,
        wasn't it?
That was *you* who took every step necessary to
        get your piece flattened
        wasn't it?

It's totally OK for you to cry:
        "He ran the red light!"
        "I'm the injured party!"
        "Why does it always happen to me!"
        "It's their fault!"

Notice, however, that you've already paid the bill.

You paid it.
And you didn't like paying it.
Now you're making it worse by
        bitching/moaning/groaning/
        feeling sorry for yourself/and
        playing right/wrong.

And it's a reaction to being ticked off about the bill.
     (Sorry)
Take a look at how effectively your cries, moans
     and bitching
     change the event.
(Doesn't work too well, does it?)

Total responsibility seems to come in stages.

Stage One:
At least take 100% responsibility
for your reaction to the event.
In other words, notice it's Response-Ability.

You can live the rest of your life
     a cripple
     feeling "un-faired" against,
     being victimized,
     or
     you can be productive, happy, and successful.
     You have
     total choice and
     total responsibility.

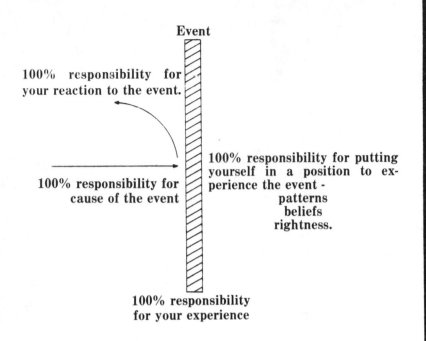

Event

100% responsibility for
your reaction to the event.

100% responsibility for putting
yourself in a position to experience the event -
        patterns
        beliefs
        rightness.

100% responsibility for
cause of the event

100% responsibility
for your experience

PERHAPS IT'S REALLY RESPONSE - ABILITY

You are totally responsible for your reaction to each event.

After each event reflect upon it:

- Has that event or a similar event ever occurred before?

- Is there a pattern?

- What do the patterns have to do with your belief systems?

- What might you be doing to set up the situation?

- What can you do to avoid negative events in the future?

- Whose responsibility is it to react in a positive manner, learn from the experience and change negative patterns?

Notice it all comes back to you.

Stage Two:

>Once you start taking 100% responsibility for
>your reaction to the event, you'll start to
>notice that you're responsible for the event itself.

>You're the one who created yourself
>in the space where the event occurred.
>Take a look and see if it has anything to do with
>>your belief systems.
>Review your tapes and see if similar events have
>>occurred in your experience before.
>Let yourself get back to the original experience.
>>Re-experience that tape,
>>this time by telling the truth about it.

>You may notice certain patterns, decisions
>>forewarnings, omens, or belief systems
>>about which you get to be right.

>There's no way out of taking responsibility
>>for your experience.
>If you aren't responsible, who is?
>>God?
>>>The Government?
>>>The President?
>>>Your Parents?
>>>Your Teachers?
>>>Your Company?
>>>The Boss?

>The only way to escape the fact of your responsibility
>>is to "unc" out.
>The problem is,
>>if you wave your ass in the breeze
>>>someone's bound to give you a close shave.
>You can't get out of responsibility
>>because you're the one with the bald ass.

>The fact that you're totally responsible for your own fate
>>doesn't negate a Higher Source.
>In fact, the more responsibility you take
>>the more you experience the reality
>>of that Higher Source.

You were given the freedom of choice -
    then you negated choice
    when you negated responsibility.

Taking total responsibility is a tough concept
        because everyone has been telling you for so long,
        that you're not responsible;
        that you are the effect of your experience.
But take a look at all the choices inherent
in any given situation:
        Look at all the things that had to
        happen for you to have this book in your
        hands right now. Who has to take ultimate
        responsibility for you reading this
        right now? (Does somebody have a gun in your
        back forcing you to read?) You had to
        set it up carefully to be here
        right now, just like I did to be here
        with you. Clever aren't we?

        Who's responsible to translate these
        concepts into meaningful behavior changes
        to make your life flow smoothly? Tell me
        that I'm responsible and I'll just laugh
        and laugh - because I may not even know you.

Why not ask yourself:
        What
            you're getting out of this experience?

What are your physical sensations?
When have you experienced those feelings before?
What do they tell you about yourself?

What emotions are you experiencing?
Are these emotions ones that you experience often?
When did you make the decision that these would be your
        "favorite emotions"?
What do your emotions tell you about you?

What attitudes do you have about yourself?
What do you feel about the others included in this event?
Are there any patterns?
What lesson should you learn from this?

Look at the event; experience your "aha's" and insights
and then do everything necessary to change the event.
Learn from it -
                    then go on.

Certain people seem to have the same, (or similar),
          events reoccur, often.
          Some people can never find a parking space.
          Some people are always in trouble.
          Some people always have rotten marriages.
          Some people always have S.O.B. bosses.

Just coincidence? Sounds like a lot of shoveling.

No coincidence.
No magic.
No luck.

If you ask yourself "How"
          you created the event in your experience,
          it may take you years to study
                    quantum physics,
          to get a sense of thought/energy transformation and
                    biogravitational
                    self organizing
                    field forces,
and then your mind may reject it all anyway.

If you ask yourself "Why"
          you created the event in your experience you may
                    a.) never figure it out,
                    b.) not know for years, the significant pieces of
                         the puzzle called your life,
                    c.) catch a terrible disease called
                         "Paralysis by Analysis"
                         (i.e. through analyzing your life, you may
                         stop living it and experiencing it. You
                         may become totally paralyzed.)

Take a look at it:
If you get killed in an "accident" it may not have been
your "fault," however, you are definitely responsible for
being dead.

At that point, it becomes a null program.
It doesn't make any difference who
        is at "fault" or to "blame."
It's like saying:
        "Goddamn it, I'm not dead!"
Except you can't say that
        when you're dead.
Or maybe you can, but no one will hear you.

If you want to play the game of life to experience satisfaction
        you need to assume that you're the cause
        of your experience.

To gain more satisfaction you may have to give up your
        Victim role.

Everybody loves to indulge themselves
        in the fantasy called,
        "Somebody is making me unhappy."
The truth is that an instant of NOW went by and
        you *chose*
        to be unhappy.

That's the way it works.
        There's no one kicking you in the ass
                to make you unhappy.
You do it to you.
You've always done it to yourself.

Without Victims,
        there are no Persecutors.
Some Victims choose to be persecuted
        just to avoid responsibility.
That's when the Rescuers enter the drama.
        Rescuers take responsibility for the Victim.
        Rescuers create and maintain others in Victim positions.
        So Rescuers can feel good about themselves.
        So Rescuers can feel superior.
        So Rescuers can assuage guilt feelings.
        So Rescuers can feel their life is meaningful.
Rescuers victimize the very people they say
        they're helping.
Rescuers rob Victims of the opportunity of getting in
        touch with what they've done to themselves.

The rest of the story is that
Victims end up resenting the people
        who rescue them.

If you're a Rescuer, stand back, because
        the Victim you save today
        may Persecute you tomorrow.

We come from a nation of Rescuers.
        We've never understood why all those
        undeveloped nations we rescued, ended up resenting us.

We can't understand why our welfare programs
        foster resentment for the very government that
        provides them.

We wonder why our kids
        don't take responsibility; and
        why they end up persecuting us
            later.

You only *serve* people
     by getting them in
     touch with their
     total responsibility
     in the matter.

That's called treating
     people with Dignity.

It's nice to let Victims in on
     the facts of Life:

     Do you know what happens if you don't get
     what you want?
          Nothing.
     Do you know who cares about that?
          Nobody...
               except you.

Once you become aware that nobody cares whether you get
what you want out of life, you'll begin to successfully
play this game called Life.

You'll finally know who's responsible for
getting what you want.

If your life isn't working out
    the way
    you want it to,
you'd
    better make it work your way
because
    if you don't
    no one really cares, but *you.*
Everyone else is too busy trying to get their
    own act
        together
    or
        they're too preoccupied with their own
        private chamber of horrors
        to worry about yours.

When you tell me that
        someone ruined your life or career,
it always is a
            lie.
Did they really "do it to you?"
Whose responsibility is it that your life
    became so screwed up?
Whose responsibility is it to see to it
    that it becomes unscrewed?

Giving up the drama -
Changing the channel -
        seems difficult because:

Our minds even function to make us right
about being the Victim and playing
        life from effect.

        We have to justify
                and
        make reasonable
        our negative experiences.

STAMP COLLECTIONS

A few years ago
          there was a phenomenon
          in which everyone was
          collecting
                    trading stamps:

Green stamps, plaid stamps, gold stamps.

The process was simple:
You went to a certain store or gas
          station.
The store gave you a certain number
          of stamps based on your purchase.
You put them in your stamp book,
          page by page.
You determined the "free" prize you
          wanted
          and
then you saved the appropriate number
          of books.
Finally, you went to the Redemption
          Center
          and
exchanged the books of stamps for
          your
          "free"
          gift.

Eric Berne noticed that people
          did the same things with their
          experiences from the past.
          We collect our past feelings
          and experiences to justify
          our behavior NOW.

People saved *psychological* trading stamps
that also come in several colors.

Lots of us love
          Brown Stamps.
          (Brown Stamps stand for exactly what you think
          Brown Stamps stand for.)

You collect a Brown Stamp
        whenever you say
        "Aw shit!"

Your alarm didn't go off?
        "Aw shit!"

You had a flat tire on the expressway.
        "Aw shit!"
Your boss called you on the carpet for a project you
                didn't finish on time.
        "Aw shit!"
You found the perfect dress in a size you *used* to be.
        "Aw shit!"

Eventually...
        you accumulate enough stamps to go to
                the Redemption Center
and get a "free" gift--
        "guilt-free."

With enough Brown Stamps
you can have a
        "guilt-free" argument,
"After all, they deserve it!"
"Look what they did to you!"
Most arguments are not concerned with
        Here Now -
They're concerned with There Then.

What happens is
        you take out all of the Brown Stamps
        that you've ever collected
and you both play a wonderful game of
        "So top that one!"

You go back two years ago with...
>"And you never got up with the kids..."
>"And just remember who paid for the car when you
>>wrecked it..."

And you keep going back and forth until you think
>you've won the award for the
>smelliest Brown Stamp Collection:
>"And you never took me to nice places when we dated."
>"And you never let me have the car."

Arguments are often
>an exchange of bad feelings -
>masquerading for love and caring.

The Brown Stamp Redemption Center also
>has "guilt-free quits" from the job.
Have you ever quit a job?
>Did you have enough Brown Stamps to justify it?
>"I didn't get the raise I wanted."
>"I wasn't invited to the office party!"
>"I worked my ass off and that's the thanks I get!"
>"That proposal sat in the pending file for three months."

You can also have a "guilt-free divorce."
    "After all, who could live with a woman like that?"
    "And then he forgot our anniversary!"
    "He never so much as lifted a finger to help with
        the kids!"

You can have a guilt-free fire-the-employee:
    "Your performance review over the past five years
        indicates..."
    "If you come to work late one more time..."
    "That's the last straw!"

You can spank your kids, "guilt-free:"
    "Now see what you made me do!"
    "I told you three times to stop that."
    "How many times do I have to tell you?"

I TOLD YOU THREE TIMES...

You can even have a "guilt-free suicide" -
    "What's the use in trying."
    "Life is shitty."
    "Nobody loves me."

All in all -
> The Brown Stamp Redemption Center has some of the
> > shittiest gifts going.
> And yet
> > You're the one saving!
> > You're the one with the collection!
> > No one is forcing you to collect Brown Stamps!

The Truth is you're so
> ethical

that your mind always pays you back -

You start to justify,
> make reasonable and
> try to be right
> > > about the most incredibly
> > > rotten experiences.

You're not even honest with the Redemption Center!

Let's say you turned in the 82 books for the guilt-free
> quit,

for which you had been diligently saving for years.

You walked up to the counter and said
> "Yes, I'd like one guilt-free quit. Here are
> my 82 books. Thank you very much."

That night you didn't know what to do without your

> collection so...

> You drove to the Redemption Center, broke in,
> and stole all 82 books back!

You just didn't know what to do without all that shit!

Notice: If you're saving shit, you start to smell.

And a lot of people don't want to be around you.

Of course, you do get to be **Right.**
> Someone told you
> > Life is shitty -
> > and you believed it.

However, no one is forcing you to save shit.
> (Or to shovel it for ten years!)

Nobody has a gun to your back saying
> "Save Shit or Else!"

Why don't you just flush your Brown Stamps? WHOOSH!

Maybe you're like the little toddler who doesn't
        want Mommy to flush the stuff.
You fear that without your Brown Stamps you
        wouldn't exist.
(Flush them and find out.)

What good can it possible do you to carry around all
        that shit?
Get the Joke:
        I think I'll save all the shit I can from a
                past that doesn't exist, so I can justify
                a shitty experience in the NOW. Then I'll
                wonder why my life feels so shitty and why
                I don't have satisfaction.

                The joke's on you.

Maybe, you should just walk up to someone and say,
        "I'd like to flush something between us."
It's that something that's been keeping you from
        experiencing that person.

Not only do you keep all the negative shit--

But your beliefs that you're not worthy can
keep you from experiencing the positive.
        If you have a basic belief--
                "If they really knew me
                they wouldn't like me." --
Then no one will be able to get close enough to
        share any of the positive things.

                        It's all a reflection of you.
                        Your ability to be positive
                                with others is a measure
                                of your own self-esteem.

The positives are the Gold Stamps.
　　　　Most of us are **not** wired to accept
　　　　gold stamps when offered.
It's as though you say:
　　　　"Oh, no thank you, I save Brown."

Someone says:	And you say:
"What a beautiful dinner."	"Oh, that's my mother's recipe."
"Good report, Johnson."	"Aw, anyone could do it."
"Congratulations!"	"Just lucky, I guess."
"You did beautifully."	"Aw, it was nothing."
"You look great!"	"Really? I've had this rag for years!

There are two magic words that allow you to accept
　　　　Gold Stamps when offered:

"Thank you."

Those two words not only allow you to collect Gold Stamps
　　　　they also allow you to give them back:
　　　　"Thank you, I really enjoy having you over,"
　　　　"Thank you. How kind of you."
　　　　"Thank you for all your assistance."

Not to acknowledge Gold Stamps is to discourage
　　　　getting them again.
People get tired of acknowledging you, only to have you
　　　　put down their acknowledgement.
　　　　Then you get to be right about no one ever giving you
　　　　Gold.

You get to be Right about the color of
        stamp you're saving.
Even if I give you a Gold Stamp, you can
        color it any color you wish. If you're
        a Brown Stamp collector and if you're a
        quart low on Brown, you can paint
        anything Brown.

        If I say, "John, your report was
                excellent!"

        You can paint it Brown by saying,
                "What did he mean by that?"

You can paint it Red for Anger
        by saying:
        "That S.O.B., if he paid me
        more, I'd turn in good reports
        all the time."

Or

You can paint it Blue for Hurt feelings by saying:
        "Doesn't he (snivel, snivel) think **all** my reports
                are good? (snivel)"

You can always see what you're looking for.

You create the Drama
        so you can justify
        collecting the stamps.

The scenes that take place
        during the Drama
            are the Games:

Psychological Games are behaviors
        -that keep us from acknowledging our
         responsibility in the matter;
        -that keep us from facing that which
         we are afraid to face;
        -that are automatic behavior patterns;
        -that keep us apart and from experiencing
         the true beauty of one another;
        that keep providing the stamps we like to collect.

Berne named some of the games, in *Games People Play:*

    "If it weren't for you..."

    "Now see what you made me do!"

    "You got me into this."

    "When I'm damn good and ready."

    "Look how hard I've tried."

    "Can't you see what you're doing to me?"

    "But I'm only trying to help you."

    "Why don't you...Yes, but..."

    "Let's you and him fight."

    "Kick me"

    "Stupid"

    "Poor me"

    "Lush"

    "Martyr"

WHY DOES THIS ALWAYS HAPPEN TO ME?

LET'S YOU AND HIM FIGHT

DEBTOR

POOR ME

YOU GOT ME INTO THIS

LUSH

HARRIED

AIN'T IT AWFUL?

YOU'LL HAVE TO TAKE ME AS I AM

NOW I'VE GOT YOU, YOU S.O.B.

LOOK HOW HARD I TRIED!

SCHLEMIEL

UPROAR

RAPE-O

NOW SEE WHAT YOU MADE ME DO!

LOOK WHAT YOU'RE DOING TO ME

MARTYR

MINE'S BETTER

WHAT WOULD THEY DO WITHOUT ME?

KICK ME

IF IT WEREN'T FOR YOU!

Games are very serious and sometimes dangerous.

There are first degree,
        second degree and
        third degree games.
Just like burns. A first degree burn is like sunburn;
A third degree burn involves skin grafting.

Third degree games usually end in
        The emergency room
        The morgue
        The courtroom
        The state prison
        The asylum

They're real, real risky.
You can easily get your piece
        taken away, maimed, or locked up.

But what is really risky,
        is not playing games.
At least when you play games, as shitty as they are,
        you know how they're all going to turn out.

But to be on stage,
        without the script,
                just being there - is risky.

To be authentically you
        is risky.
To play games, to run out your act, is not so risky.

Some people will like your act,
        some won't.
        But at least you can always
        hide behind your act.

The sad part is that even if other people
        like your act,
        they won't even know who
        you are.

SOME PEOPLE MAY NOT LIKE THE WAY YOU ARE

When you're just being who you are,
  some people will like you
    and some people won't.
The good part is
  those people who like you
    will really like *you.*

To just be who you are;
  won't create a lot of drama -
  just a lot of satisfaction.

To be someone you're not
  is not only schizophrenic
  it is very energy-draining.

It's like being on stage 24 hours a day
living the drama you're creating
 with no curtain call 'til the end.

To be who you are
  is to give up the drama,
    the stamps,
    the games,
    the act,

  to gain

    your own life.

Who knows? It just may be worth it.

VIII.   ABOUT SATISFACTION—
GETTING A LITTLE

The basic difference
        between those who acknowledge their responsibility
            and those
        who don't
is
        those who do
        smile more.
They have something called
        Satisfaction.

And isn't that what we're all after?

Our society has lots
      of notions and beliefs
      about what will make us happy.
But the basic belief is that it
      all boils down to

$$$$$$$$$$$$$$$

Our society and most of our institutions
      implicitly or explicitly
      tell us that money will make us happy
         But will it?
      What will money buy?
Food, clothing, shelter.

What else?

Transportation, recreation, education, luxuries (toys),
health services, power, status, entertainment, cosmetic beauty,
      leisure time.

The list could go on.
      But let's stop here.

The list is long enough
      to expose the greatest belief system
         that runs our society:

"MORE IS BETTER"

Wherever you are on the money scale,
      you probably think those people above you have it
         "wired up right."

So you constantly strive to earn more money.
You say,
> "If I could only get a raise.
then
> I would be happy."

And what that notion does
> is to keep you constantly on the
> treadmill.

IS MORE BETTER?

Maybe,

  --just maybe--

   More isn't Better.

Maybe, More is just

   More.

That's all.

And less is just less.

   Not worse.

Is more money really better
   than less money?

   Are rich people happier than poor people?
   Are poor people happier than rich people?
   (I know, rich people are supposed to be miserable...

   I have some bad news:
   There are some happy rich people in this universe.
     It doesn't seem fair,
     but that's just the way it is.)

And there are some happy, poor people.
And some miserable rich and unhappy poor.

Maybe happiness really isn't wired to money.

Money isn't satisfaction;
   it's just convenience.

Is more food better than less food?

In order to be a good boy or girl
do you really have to finish everything on your plate?

Does it really make the people in China/
India/Europe/Biafra
any happier because you're wearing the food they
may lack?
Are expensive restaurants always better than less
expensive restaurants?

Is more clothing better than less clothing?
Many of us have our happiness wired
to our next
suit
dress
coat
shoes
fur

We have this belief that "it" will make us happy.

And then we get "It."

We wear it once and
- *zap* -
No more satisfaction.
Now it's old.

How about luxuries?
How many
diamonds,
stereos,
motorcycles,
campers,
swimming pools,
paintings
will it take before you become happy?

How many operations is it going to take
before you're happy?
How many pills will it take?

Is the president of the company more
satisfied than the clerk typist
in the secretarial pool?

Is more power better than less power?
Ask Richard M. Nixon.

Is more entertainment better?
Go to Las Vegas.
Notice the
overwhelming sense of joy
as the people rush frantically to
"take it all in."
How many
shows,
movies,
rodeos,
plays,
operas,
will it take to make
you
happy?

Is more beauty better than
less beauty?
Is it possible to be beautiful
and happy?
(Yes, damn it. And it doesn't seem fair.
The bad news is some people are rich, beautiful and happy!)

Is it possible to be homely and happy? Of course.

Does more money given to the
        church
        provide a more secure place in heaven?

Is a more expensive church or
        temple better than a less
        expensive one?

Religion is simply that
        experience of God
            from within you.

Don't confuse that experience
        with the institution
        that attempts to offer the
        space for that to occur.

Is more education
        better
        than
        less education?

The belief system is that you have to obtain a degree
        in order to be happy.

"If only I had a (College Education,
                a master's degree, or a doctorate...)
                then I could be happy."

Notice the groups that have the greatest rate of suicide
and divorce are the professionals with lots of education.

Maybe education doesn't make you happy.
There are plenty of miserable people with degrees,
        and there are plenty of happy people with degrees.

Perhaps education is not better or worse.
        Education is just education.

What about shelter?

Know anyone who feels that
if we could just get a larger apartment or home we'd
be happy?
If we could just buy a vacation house/a larger lot/
add more rooms/
live in a more expensive neighborhood/then we'd be happy?

Is more transportation better?
Are people in chauffeured limousines
happier than people in beat-up Volkswagens?
Are people who own three cars happier than those
people who don't own one?
Are the first class passengers happier than the
coach passengers?
And take a look at how crazy this is.
"More is Better" is literally choking us
to death.

Is more recreation better than less?
How many times do you need to go
skiing?
camping?
golfing to make you happy?

Some go often and they're happy
Some don't go at all and they're happy.

Is large government better than
        small government?
                (Silly question!)

Are more friends better than few friends?

Is more sex better than less sex?
Ever know anyone getting lots of
        Sex,
        without any
        Satisfaction
                and vice-versa?

Like Eric Hoffer says:

"YOU CAN NEVER GET ENOUGH OF WHAT YOU
REALLY
        DON'T NEED TO MAKE YOU HAPPY.

Going the other extreme
        doesn't work either.
Less is not better.

The Less-Betters
are people who reject
        money and materialism.

They go around saying,
        "I just have my jeep and my dawg!"

Most less-betters grew up in
        more-better homes.

Mr. and Mrs. More Better
        had a son, named
                Les Better
and Les moved West
        to find himself.
He thought
        that if he gave up everything his
                parents had,
                        he would be happy.

He felt that materialism and money
        did it to them.
The sad part was that
        Les didn't find happiness either.

Materialism - more or less - has little to do with
        satisfaction.

Money won't make you happy or frustrated.
Money is just money.
        It is simply convenient to have it.
        That's all.

It won't make you a better person or
        more satisfied with your experience of life.
It won't solve your problems for you.

Most of us have been playing
        More is Better
for so long,
        (and there's so much agreement that it's right to play it,)
that we never bothered to look into our own experience
to find out if that's where satisfaction is.

You can't play the game of
        Materialism
                and
        have fun,
as long as your "More is Better" belief system
        stays intact.
However, as soon as
        you're satisfied from within yourself,
        then you can choose
        to play
        MATERIALISM and
        have a ball.

You'll soon notice that it's all just a game
and the purpose of the game is to have fun,
        not to prove that you're better
                or more important.

        It's just to have fun.

So it's OK to have more or less
        it doesn't matter;
just have fun and gain some satisfaction in the process.

Some of us have a belief
        that we can't have satisfaction
        until we've reached our goal,
        or achieved what we set out to achieve.

Notice what happens with that.
        We moan and groan
        until we reach our goal.

If we don't reach our goal
        we're miserable.

If we do -
        we're happy...
        But for how long?
                Until the novelty wears off?
                Until we set our next goal?
                Maybe we're just relieved, from the alleviation
                        of the Panic it took to get there.

When we have Satisfaction
        wired only to achievement
        or the end result
we don't get to experience it
        very often.

It's great to realize that you
can be satisfied in the process of attaining your goals.

How often is it possible
        to experience
                Satisfaction?

Anytime
        you're willing to
                accept
        what's going on in your experience NOW.

Satisfaction
        is a
        Choice
        that's made

        NOW.

Satisfaction
        comes from
        Experiencing what's happening

        Consciously
                and
        Accepting
                the
        Perfection
                of it
                        ALL.

Who determines your satisfaction...?

Who else could?

Get the joke
        when someone tells you
        that you
                should be happy?

You either
        are
        or
        you're not.
        (You've stepped in it - or you haven't)

If you wait for happiness to happen to you
        you may wait for a long time.

An ancient Chinese proverb says:
        "Starving man wait long time
        for roast duck to fly into mouth."

You are
        the only one
                who can determine whether you're happy.

No one
        and
nothing can do it for you.

It is your
        fundamental responsibility
                to produce
                        satisfaction
                                for yourself.

How do you get Satisfaction?

Be Conscious: If you think of times you experienced
happiness, joy, inner peace and satisfaction,
were you *there* for it? Of course. In
order to experience Satisfaction it takes
Aliveness.

Share the truth: Satisfaction in a relationship stems from
true communication. To communicate we need
to share our experience of self with another
and be willing to experience the other person
the way they are.

You can have relationships of
                    convenience and
                    co-existence;
But to have love and satisfaction
                    you have to
                    share the truth.

Satisfaction is present
                    to the same degree
                    to which you tell the
                                        truth
                                        in your
                                        relationship.

Accept your experience of NOW as Perfect:

According to Webster, Perfect is
(1) "a state proper to a thing when
completed; having all the essential elements,
characteristics, etc. (2) in a state of
complete excellence; faultless, unflawed."

To experience satisfaction
you simply have to
acknowledge
the perfection of your experience -
even with those things you don't like.

Satisfaction is being conscious
        sharing the truth,
        noticing the perfection of your experience,
        and
        accepting total responsibility.

To be dissatisfied
        is to be playing tapes,
        telling lies or withholding the truth,
        bitching
        and
        assuming no responsibility in the matter.

Dissatisfaction comes in many unconscious forms:

fear	jealousy
hostility	bitching
anger	blaming
envy	frustration
boredom	embarrassment
tiredness	reasonableness
rightness	hoping
wishing	trying
lying	withholding

Using English
        we have a hard time describing
                Love, Truth, Happiness, Satisfaction.

        But notice
                the list of unconsciousness could go on forever.

Eskimos have many words for snow -
        because they live in it.
We have no trouble describing negative forms of unconsciousness
        because we live in it.

You and only you are the source of your
        satisfaction
                and
        dissatisfaction.

You have total choice in the matter.

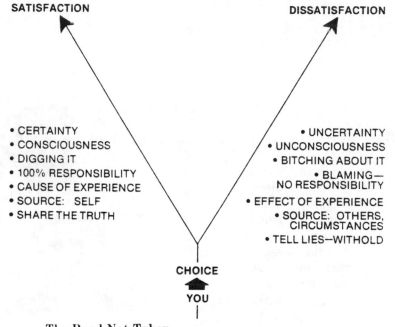

SATISFACTION   DISSATISFACTION

- CERTAINTY
- CONSCIOUSNESS
- DIGGING IT
- 100% RESPONSIBILITY
- CAUSE OF EXPERIENCE
- SOURCE: SELF
- SHARE THE TRUTH

- UNCERTAINTY
- UNCONSCIOUSNESS
- BITCHING ABOUT IT
- BLAMING— NO RESPONSIBILITY
- EFFECT OF EXPERIENCE
- SOURCE: OTHERS, CIRCUMSTANCES
- TELL LIES—WITHOLD

CHOICE

YOU

The Road Not Taken

Two roads diverged in a wood, and I-
I took the one less traveled by
and that has made all the difference.

—Robert Frost

You are the source of your satisfaction and dissatisfaction. And you
have total choice in the matter. There's a fork in the road and you
get to choose.

The road to satisfaction is
        an express lane.
Very few are dedicated to experience satisfaction in their lives.

The road to dissatisfaction is
        bumper to bumper.

All the agreement is
        on the side of dissatisfaction.

If you're wondering
        whether you're satisfied...
If you have to ask the question
        you already have the answer.

How long will it take
        before you give yourself
                the freedom to be happy?

You can only be satisfied
        Here Now.
That's all you have.

                Our mind loves to delay our satisfaction
                or to make it a future condition.

                "I was happy when..."
                "I will be happy..."
                "If only...then I would be happy..."

NOW is the only space from whence we get to play.
Just look at your experience and
        tell the truth about it.

Telling the truth about yourself
        produces satisfaction and direction.

Satisfaction is
        where you want it,
        when you want it,
        how you want it.

Just let it be
        and
be there with it.

**THE ROAD TO DISSATISFACTION
IS BUMPER TO BUMPER**

IX.   ABOUT MAKING AND KEEPING AGREEMENTS

Once we know
        what we want, then all we have to do
        is to set up the machinery to get it.
The machinery
        has to do with formulating and keeping
                commitments.

An agreement is a commitment to produce a result.

If you want to produce a result with someone,
first, you'll have to agree upon the result that you want
        to accomplish,
        then, you'll have to tell the truth about it,
        and finally, you'll have to do what's necessary to get it.

The Dance

Once you're aware of how the universe is set up, it's like directing a very well-rehearsed orchestra---
When it's time for the violins to come in, the violins come in.
You don't have to beg, coax, or demand; you simply direct the action.

In order for your life to work, it must be based on agreements.
Your relationships,
your job,
your company,
your marriage,
all produce satisfaction to the extent that you make and keep your agreements.

Not to keep agreements is to become the effect of the relationship. You get to be right and dissatisfied.

A neurotic is a person who makes agreements with himself and then breaks them.
Neurotic behavior is to make agreements with others with no intention of keeping them.

You pay yourself back for not keeping your agreements.
You can make a lot of money and not keep agreements,
You can have lots of possessions, be famous,
be respected and not keep agreements
You can have it all and have nothing.
The bottom line is satisfaction:
Yours.
You either have it or you don't.
How long are you going to continue to
lie to yourself?

If you don't have satisfaction
in your relationship,
on your job,
with your friends...
there's a lie.
Look for the broken agreement.

Remember that people don't break agreements *on* you,
only *with* you.

The truth is *you* are.
If you notice a lot of dissatisfaction and broken
agreements
with others--
rather than blaming *them,*
you'd better ask yourself, what you're getting out
of the situation.
Why do you have people in your experience that
break agreements with you?
Maybe you don't need to play the Victim of broken
agreements.

If you have broken agreements
look for the underlying truth.

In order for an agreement to work,
it has to be perceived as being mutually beneficial.
Otherwise, no result is produced.

A relationship that only serves one person doesn't last.

Remember that the stake we're playing for
    is not the result itself.
The stake we're playing for
    is the sense of satisfaction.
And that makes it alright to go ahead and play
    to produce results.

The basis of an agreement is the
    truth.
If you don't tell the truth, take a look at
    who gets damaged.

If you really want to do damage to yourself,
    blame the other person for not producing the result.
    Lie about your responsibility in the matter.

Look at the illusion
    that a partnership is
    a 50-50 proposition.
There you sit saying,
    "Well, I did my 50%, where's his?"

Playing it from 50-50
    just doesn't work.
    The problem is that if your partner falls down
    you have to pay the bill.
There just ain't no 50-50 in the universe...not from where *you* sit.

You'll get 100% of whatever you're willing to take responsibility
    for getting.

If you enter into an agreement and your partner lies,
what you'll notice is that you set it up for your
partner to lie.
Then you lied to yourself when you refused to look at it.

The only thing that can't lie is the result.

All you have to do is to look at the result you said you
were committed to producing,
and that'll tell you if one or both of you have been lying.

When you let a broken agreement slide, through hoping and
wishing, you may begin to notice that you've been
withholding and lying,
and you just gave up your satisfaction.

Playing from the truth
doesn't seem easy
until you do it.
Then it will become obvious that there's
no other way to play

It isn't that it's wrong to lie. It just doesn't work.

Everytime you tell a lie, it'll rob you of your satisfaction.
If you enter into an agreement that
you're unwilling to keep
it'll be like a boomerang thrown into the universe.
It'll hit you on the head every time.

Let's look at a common example:
I ask Mary to lunch with me on Wednesday at 12:00 noon
in the new Italian Villa restaurant. Because it's close
to where she works, she agrees to meet me there.

We have an agreement to produce a mutually beneficial
result:

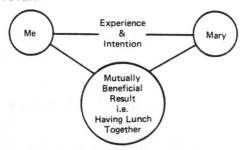

On Wednesday I show up at 12:00 and
          Guess What? No Mary!

My typical response would be to
     bitch,
          blame,
               moan,
                    groan,
                         worry,
                              reach for my stamp book
                              and make Mary wrong.

(Notice that to blame others
          is
               to create a new automatic response
                         or
               to reinforce old ones.)

How much responsibility do I take
          for Mary not showing?
          --O--Zero--None--Zilch--

          ("Well, I was there on time! I kept my part
          of the agreement! I put in my 50%.")

What's the truth?
          I am totally responsible for my reaction
          to the event. I am also responsible for
          the event itself. I didn't do everything
          necessary to produce the result.

She didn't do it to me.
I did it to me.

I did everything necessary
          for the situation to be exactly
               the way it was.

Am I at fault or
          am I to blame?

No, I am just the cause.

Fault and blame are really asking whether you are wrong.

Being the cause is neither being right or wrong.

To find fault or to identify blame
        is just an evaluation of the event.
And if you think about it,
        evaluations are useless chatter.
Often after the event passes,
        after a moment, month, or year,
           we'll notice the perfection of an event
           that originally we judged to be
              awful, frightening, terrible.
To be cause
        is to notice the perfection
        at the instant of its occurrence.

The experience of Mary not showing up is perfect.
It's just hard to realize that when
        you're playing from effect.
To determine that you are cause, ask,
        "Did I do *everything* necessary to produce the result?"

Results don't lie.

        I didn't call to remind her.
        I didn't pick her up.
        I didn't tell her that lunch was "on me."
        I didn't tell her exactly where I would meet her.
        I didn't tell her how important lunch was for me.
        I didn't make certain she was conscious when I made
           the agreement.

And maybe when things like that happen to you,
        you should ask yourself
        "What do I get out of having it be this way?"

Maybe
        you get to make Mary wrong,
           because she made you wrong once. (Retaliation)
or
        you get to feel sorry for yourself,
           "Why does this always happen to me?"
or
        you get to manifest your belief systems:
           "Just like a woman to forget about lunch!"

There are all kinds of reasons you'd
        do that to you,
                and you're the only one who knows the truth.

And do you want to know the real
        kick in the kimono?

You both knew when you made the agreement
        that it wouldn't work.

Somehow I knew she would
        stand me up and so did she.

You know when you're making an agreement
        whether it's the truth
                        or
                        not,
                        or
                whether you're both lying.

It makes total nonsense
        out of playing the game.

You typically know at the time that you
        have no intention
        of keeping the agreement.

        You know that the agreement is
                unreasonable or just
                wishful thinking.

        Or something just tells you,
                "It'll never work."

When you think of times
        when you kept your agreement --
        when you produced the result --
        when you did it --
Didn't you know you'd do it when
        you made the agreement?

And when you didn't keep the agreement...
        didn't you know when you made the agreement
                in the first place?

When did you know the marriage wouldn't work?
       ("Oh, before we got married.")

When did you know that this wasn't the right
               job for you?
       ("Oh, before I was hired.")

When did you know that you shouldn't finish
               the task?
       ("Oh, when I told myself I would.")

What a joke!

At work your boss asks
       if you can produce a thousand widgets
And you say,
       "Sure."
               (And the voice inside your head is going nuts --
               "You'll never be able to do that!"
               "A thousand widgets, he must be
               crazy!")

That's called Management by Wishes.

"Can you produce 1000 widgets?"

       "Sure *wish* I could, boss."

"I sure *wish* you could too!"

And then you spend the rest of the year
       trying,
       efforting,
       and
       coming up with excuses,
               justifications,
                       reasonableness,
                               and rightness!

Life
       is
       Results
               or
                       Bullshit.

You are
        either producing the results one time, as agreed,
        or
        you're producing the bullshit
        as to why you haven't produced the results.

Bullshit comes packaged in many forms:
        reasonableness,
        belief systems,
        excuses,
        justifications,
        being right,
        blaming other people,
                circumstance,
                        or events.

The instant you comprehend
        that you've lied
                about the agreement,
you immediately start
        to blame
                and
        assign cause elsewhere.
                                It's not a very fun game.

Results lead to satisfaction,
                        completeness,
                        fulfillment.

Bullshit leads to more Bullshit.
        And it's all Uncing out.

It's all Theater of the Absurd
        when you realize that...
                companies spend more time and energy
                producing Bullshit rather than the results
                they said they wanted.
                And everyone knew that it was all
                going to turn into Bullshit at
                the beginning of the process.

        It's as though everyone said,
                "Let's create Bullshit,
                Lie about it,
                go Unconscious together,
                and get paid in the process."

It's totally amazing
        that some companies survive.

A COMMITTEE CREATING B.S.

Bullshit takes hours,
                and hours,
                          and hours.
If you can't come up with enough
        justifications
        and excuses yourself,
                you can formulate a committee to help you.
A committee is a B.S. producing machine.

If you're producing results,
    there's not much to talk about except to say:
        "We did it!"

If you're not producing results,
    "Oh my God, the excuses, the rightness,
    the justifications, the reasonableness,
    you can come up with..."
It takes hours,
    and becomes very dramatic
        since it's all effect.

Sales people who are producing results
    don't have time for meetings and conferences
        with their managers.
Those who aren't producing results,
    need a lot of management time to bitch about
        bad leads,
        flaky customers,
        bad time of the year,
        poor training,
        bad sales tools,
        "nobody homes"
        too few ads,
        etc.
        etc.
        etc.

According to Lao Tzu in 600 B.C.,
    "Those who know don't talk.
    Those who talk don't know."

We accept responsibility
    when we're producing results and
keeping our agreements.
    "Did you do everything necessary
    to produce the result?"
Of course, or you wouldn't have the result.

And when we are not producing results and not keeping our
    agreements, we scream "I'm not responsible!"

Your mind resists
    the 100% responsibility clause. It doesn't like it.
However, this is not a ploy to convince you;
    it's just a report on how the universe works.

Everytime you made an agreement
and it worked
both parties took 100% responsibility,
(i.e.,did everything necessary to produce the result)
to make it work.

How long are you going to lie
about having no responsibility
when the agreement doesn't work?

Every time you lie
you produce more Bullshit
for you to shovel.
You produce so much yourself,
you don't need any help
from the four-legged "moo" varieties.

A manager from a large life insurance agency
just didn't want to acknowledge his 100% responsiblity.
He said that if he had ten agents
who made an agreement to each have
a million dollar sales year,
that he would make an agreement
with his boss for ten million dollars in
volume for his office.

He really had trouble seeing
how *he* was responsible if
they broke their agreements.

Aspect the reverse:
If they did keep their agreements,
would he take responsibility for them producing the
results?
You betcha!
He would have done everything necessary
to insure that the results were produced --
He would have
worked with the agents who were have
problems,
provided special incentives,
held weekly meetings and progress reviews,
presented special sales seminars,
insured good, qualified leads, etc.....

He would have well deserved the pat on his back from his boss.

What about when the result wasn't produced?
It was *their* fault!
  (Keep shoveling!)
The truth would be that he did absolutely
  everything necessary *not* to produce the result
    He didn't
      work with the agents who were having
      problems,
      provide special incentives,
      etc., etc., etc.

You are totally responsible
  for everything in your experience.

Your intention is your experience.
  Your experience is your intention.

Yeah, but...
  How can I be responsible
    for the computer breaking down?
    for the building burning?
    for my boss quitting?
    for the vendor going on strike?

The question isn't "How?"
  unless you're big on
    biogravitational self-organizing field forces
    and quantum physics.

The question is "What?"
  "What am I getting out of having it be this way?"
  "What can I learn from this experience?"

Bitching doesn't change the negative
    It
only makes it reasonable to self and others.

In order for life to work smoothly,
  it takes you doing what's necessary to keep
    your agreements with yourself and others
  and promoting relationships with others that
    are mutually beneficial.

X. ABOUT GETTING WHAT YOU WANT AND WANTING WHAT YOU GET

People play games to see if they can win.
Some of us play life the same way.
        The only thing wrong with that is
        that you think you have to win to
                experience satisfaction.

What about the rest of the time you're playing life?

Life is like a chart
        that goes up and down.
It has peaks and valleys.
That's the drama we create with a series of Nows.

Playing to win
        is drawing an arbitrary line
                and saying
                        "I'll be happy at that point."

Notice that a "win"
        only lasts one instant of Now.
So if you're playing to win,
        you're using up all your time
        to get one instant of satisfaction.
"Wins" may not come too often.

So how can you
        change it to make more sense?
The first step is
        to set a goal.

Goals produce results.
Results produce satisfaction.

You can't get that which you don't know you want.

What you want could be out there
in the universe
and you wouldn't recognize it.
If you are unclear about your goals
you don't have any.
What you have are
wishes
not
goals.

To accomplish your goals you must have
clarity.
As long as you think your wishes
are your goals
you won't be able to reach them.

THERE'S A DIFFERENCE BETWEEN
A GOAL AND A WISH!
BE SPECIFIC!

In order to get what you want,

get

<u>S</u>
<u>M</u>
<u>A</u>
<u>R</u>
<u>T</u>

about your goals.

For a goal to be a goal, and not a wish, it must be:

Specific:
Until a goal is specific, it doesn't require
concrete action.
>"I'd like to lose some weight," doesn't
>>get the job done.
>"I want to increase productivity," is
>>a wish.

Getting specific avoids future bitching. If
I tell my secretary to buy a new chair for
the office, she could buy an upholstered
chair or a typing chair, and then I could
bitch that,
>"I didn't want *that* kind of chair!"
Wishes have no reality, no substance. If
you want to get what you want, be as specific
as possible.

BE SPECIFIC!

Measurable: To determine whether you've accomplished
your goal, it must be measurable. Making
it measurable lets you know whether you've
accomplished it. Notice the difference
between
>"I'd like to lose some weight," and
>"I'm going to lose three pounds this week."

Acceptable: To be acceptable, both the goal and the means
to accomplish the result must be ethical.
      "I'm going to lose three pounds next
      week by taking diuretics and speed,"
      is not acceptable.
      "I'm going to have $3,000.00 in the
      bank next year," is a fine goal unless
      you plan to embezzle the money.
We are totally ethical beings. Responsibility
brings together all of your moral and ethical
considerations.
      The end does not justify the means.
There's nothing wrong with
      lying; cheating and stealing.
They just don't work.
      They won't produce what we want the
      goal to produce -
        - what we're after -
          satisfaction.
You may find that you are unwilling to do
      what's necessary to produce the result,
        if the result or the means are
        unethical (and you always know).

Realistic: If you have unrealistic goals,
      who are you kidding?
Look what happens:
      "I want to lose ten pounds next week,"
        and then you only lose three.
      All that does is allow you to feel badly
      that you didn't accomplish the goal.
People who set realistic goals for themselves,
      and then accomplish those goals,
      feel good about themselves.
People who set their goals too high,
      feel badly when they don't reach them.
People who set their goals too low,
      feel badly, because
        "Anybody coulda done it."

Some have it wired
      to win when they lose,
      to lose when they win.
Why not win when you win?

Truth: Is the goal the Truth?
                You
                    are
the only one who knows for certain.
If the goal isn't the truth,
                it will get stuck in your tube
                and
                once again, you'll suffer from
                                cosmic constipation.

The process of becoming
                *S*pecific,
                *M*easurable,
                *A*cceptable,
                *R*ealistic,
                *T*ruthful
        is taking responsibility for the goal.

And that is smart.

There's just no way
        to take responsibility for what is beneficial
                until you know what you want.
The sense of satisfaction
        comes from telling the truth
                about what you want
                        and
                doing what's necessary to get it.

The second thing you
                have to do to get what you want
                        is
                to determine whether you have the *ability*
                        to accomplish the goal you've set for
                        yourself.

You either
        have it
            or
        you don't.
                That s all there is to say about your ability.

How do you know
    whether you have the ability?
    You know it
        like you know the Truth.

Perhaps you like to play from
    "Poor little me, I just don't have the
        ability."
    Notice how effectively that helps you
        avoid responsibility.
    We were all born with incredible
        ability, we've just managed to
        cover it with a phenomenal amount
            of B.S.

"I don't think I have the ability,"
    is a tape
    that keeps you from finding out
        whether you do or you don't.
    It allows you to play from
        5%-20%-40%-60%-80%-90%

The fear is
    that if you put 100% of *you* out there,
    it may not be enough!

    And if you fail you might get embarrassed!
    You might not get everyone's approval.

Don't worry about it.
    You have an incredible amount of ability.
    You have all the ability you need.

Everytime you're willing,
    you'll find the ability necessary
        to accomplish the result.
    That is, unless you're addicted to B.S.

The B.S. makes a wish out of a goal.
You create a wish when you say you have a goal and
    you don't have the ability to accomplish it.

Let's say your goal is to win
    a five mile marathon jogging race.
    That sounds like a good goal
        until you state that you're in a wheelchair.
        "Poof!"
    The goal just became a wish.

A lot of people play life wishing from wheelchairs.

So, if you are
    S M A R T
about your goals and
    if you have the
        ability -
            all you have to do is
                    Do It!

To accomplish a goal -
    to get what you want -
        you have to take RESPONSIBILITY.

Who's responsible for the achievement of a goal?
    The myth is that it depends on other people.
    (And we all know what that's all about!)

The only scarce commodity
    in the universe is people
        willing to take total
            responsibility.

The test to determine whether you're willing
      to take responsibility
          is
      to ask yourself
          "Am I willing to do what's necessary to
          accomplish the goal?"

"Yes" or "No."
      Not "Almost"
      Not "Maybe"
      Not "To a certain extent."

The only way
      to get what you want
          is
      for you to do everything
          necessary to
            Get it.

            Get it?

It only can work that way.
      The rest of the B.S. is not only ridiculous,
          but utter nonsense.

You've probably been waiting for
          good luck
      for a long time.
      It just hasn't seemed to materialize.

Funny,
      the instant you take responsibility
      for what you want,
      somehow you get "lucky" as hell!!
      You become tremendously "Fortunate."

According to Campbell,
    "People who want milk should not seat themselves
    on a stool in the middle of a field in hopes that
    a cow will back up to them."

               You have to do everything
                 necessary.
                     Everything.

When you first state a goal
    you say, "I want that."
    In order to get it,
        you have to start on the path of doing everything
        that's required to get it.

What happens if you stop half-way?
    You won't get it.
    No matter what else is going on.
    If you stop at 99%
        it's no result.

Everything means *everything.*

For example,
I'm a lousy skier,
I ski by tumbling down mountain sides.
Now I might tell myself that I have a goal
of becoming an expert skier in two years.
Do I have the ability?
The answer is clearly "yes."

Am I willing to do everything necessary
in order to accomplish the goal?
The answer is "no."
I'm not willing to take ski instructions,
to go out on the slopes every weekend,
to buy good equipment,
to stand in the long lines, etc.
Therefore,
my goal just became a wish:
"I sure wish I could become an expert skier."

Everytime
you set something as
a goal
and it's really a wish,
it gets stuck in your tube.

It's much easier to tell the truth
about it now at the beginning of the process
than to get it stuck.
Why even start the process?

Don't start
        things that you're unwilling
        to take responsibility for completing.

Why not set the universe up to
        serve
            you?

When you tell the truth about what you want,
        you create it.
You don't get stuck in it.

When you bitch about it,
        or say that someone or something else is responsible,
            Life gets real
                heavy.

If what you're doing doesn't work,
        you've got to ask,
            "What's the source of the problem?"
            "What are all the belief systems (B.S.) between me
            and having it be the way I say I'd like it to be?"

    "Woulda"
            "Coulda"
                "Shoulda"
                        are ridiculous statements.
The idea that you could have done something
        that you didn't,
            is psychotic.

Perhaps you have a belief system
        that you have to "effort"
        at accomplishing a goal.

TRYING IS NOT DOING

"Trying" is usually an excuse
for not doing.

It is a concept employed to justify self-defeat.
Have you ever "tried" to get to sleep at night?
    The harder you try, the more awake you become.
Have you ever "tried" to lose weight?
    All you're saying is you're efforting at what you're
        not doing.
Have you ever "tried" to quit smoking?
    "Trying to quit" means you're still smoking,
        and efforting like hell not to.

In the real world there are no "A's" for effort,
    only for producing results.

If you think you're working your ass off,
    turn around and
        check if it's still there.

Perhaps you have a belief system that says,
"I never have enough time..."

This is an inaccurate statement.
You have all the time there is.
No one in the universe
has more time than you do.

You never *have* time.
You *create* time.
You choose to do what's necessary during that period.

Maybe you like to run the tape,
"I just can't afford it."

There's no scarcity of money in the universe.
There's more money than you could possibly spend.
"Can't" typically translates into
"Won't."

When you say
"I can't"
you're putting the responsibility outside of self.

"I won't..." assumes responsibility and choice.
"Can't afford," means, "I won't do whatever is necessary
to produce the result."
"I just can't talk to
my boss,
my spouse,
my kid,
my parents,
equates to
"I won't do what's necessary to
communicate effectively."
"I won't get off my position."

Stop lying to yourself
and to others about it.

A COMMITTEE MAKING
DECISIONS OVER COFFEE

Maybe you have a belief system
that you need a group decision
and then no one is willing to stick their neck out.

When no one takes responsibility
        for decision-making or producing results
        no one gets to do what he wants.

It's total nonsense
        to persist in an activity that doesn't produce results.

You need to ask yourself
        "How many times have I done things that haven't
        been loyal to my purpose?"

It takes a lot of careful,
           unconscious planning to
                screw it up,
                     and
                feel justified about it.
The truth is
you get what
you get what
           you unconsciously
                intended to get.

Not to get
           what you said you wanted
                is to have
                     lied
                about your prior intention.

To become conscious about your
intentions
           is to make happen
                what's happening, directionally.

To get
           what you truly
                intend to get...

                Clarify your goals.
                     Be SMART about them,
                     check to see if you have the ability,
                     and take responsibility
                          of making it happen.

That's when your life starts to expand
           because
                responsibility involves the awareness,
                     that you choose every moment of Now.

Coming from a position of choice
           allows you the freedom
                to be
                     who you are -
                          and who you are
                                to become.

IF YOU DON'T KNOW WHERE YOU'RE GOING, YOU
CAN'T GET THERE, AND YOU CAN'T GET
ANYWHERE UNTIL YOU KNOW WHO YOU ARE.

- SENECA

XI. ABOUT MAKING RELATIONSHIPS WORK

A Relationship
        is a series of agreements
        to produce results.
            The best relationships
                produce Satisfaction.

In any Relationship, it's important to ask:
        What do I want out of this Relationship?
        What am I willing to put into it?

For the Relationship to last
        the answer to those questions needs to balance.
Expect too much,
            without giving,
        and you'll go unconscious with
            Blame, Disappointment & Frustration.
Give more than you're getting
        And you'll go unconscious with
            Resentment, Wishes, and Hopes.

If you're not getting enough from your relationships-
            at work, with your spouse, with your children,
                from your friends-
Then you're probably playing from effect:
        They're doing it to you or not doing it for you,
        And you keep waiting for it all to happen to you.

To be the Effect of your Relationship
        is to produce B.S. rather than Satisfaction.
        Of course, the B.S.
            does give you something to talk about
                over coffee, at cocktail parties, on golf
                courses
        If your relationships are working,
            there's not much to say.
            If your shoes fit, you don't feel them.

All you have to do to get the relationship to work
        is to take responsibility
            for what's happening.

Just take responsibility for what's going on already
        and you've won.

It's very simple.

If you assume
                cause
        rather than
                effect
        in your relationships,
you may be able to experience
                                satisfaction
        throughout the relationship
                                in   ups
                        both   and
                                the   downs.

Relationships are
        two sided-you and me.
When you enter into a relationship,
        you must accept it as 100%-100%,
                                        not 50%-50%.

You have to take responsibility for the other person.
        as well as yourself.
        To say, "Well, that's their problem"
                is a nasty little joke. Look again.

You may not like it that way.
        That's just the way it is.

If you enter into a relationship and say,
        "I have no control over my partner."
        That's a lie.
And you know it's a lie
        because when the bill comes due,
        guess who pays it!

If your partner doesn't do
    what *you* want,
    it's your experience that suffers.
So if you want your relationship to serve you,
        you must be willing to reach out
        and take the 100% responsibility you have
            to make it work.

Once you realize that you created the situation
        exactly the way it is right now,
you'll also notice the
        person with whom you have the relationship
            is exactly
        the person you asked
                            Central Casting
            to send over.

The person doesn't have to change in order to be who they are.

Take a look at how much energy
        we put into getting the other
        person to change--
                (Not too effective, is it?)

You'll always be miserable
        as long as you're bitching or blaming
        the other person
            for what you're experiencing.
    Too often we demand that the other person change
        and then bitch when they don't.

**IT'S EASIER TO RIDE THE HORSE IN THE DIRECTION
IT'S GOING** —*Werner Erhard*

Waiting for the other person to change
    allows you to be right.

Being right may destroy the relationship.
    You always lose.
    Even if you win, you lose.
        because you get to play alone...
           And that's why you entered the relationship
             in the first place--
             so you wouldn't have to play alone.

Right/Wrong
    are really two sides of the same coin.
It doesn't make any difference
    who's right and who's wrong.
If the result of being satisfied
    is not produced,
        you're both lying.
And there's no right or wrong in that.
Who says what's right and what's wrong,
    and does any of it matter if you're not satisfied?

In your original agreement, you said,
    "I want to work with -
           -love-
           -be with- you."

Not
    "I want to be right when I'm with you."

If you and I are fighting
      and both of us are unwilling to stop fighting
            nothing will happen.
      Neither of us is willing to move from our
            position of rightness.

To get relationships to work,
      you have to be willing to play from a position
            other than Right/Wrong.

Take a look at what might happen
      if you just unilaterally–
            (without asking anybody for anything;)
            (without asking your partner to do anything;)
      communicated the truth about what was going on.

      All you'd have to do is give up your position
            about being right.

Not being Right will allow you to experience your
            relationship from
      a Cause position.

To assume Cause of what's happening in your relationship
      is to acknowledge
            that you had total choice all along;
            that you are getting something out of having the
                  relationship be the way it is;
            that you have choice right now
                  to continue the relationship as is,
                      or
                  to change within the relationship,
                      or
                  to end the relationship.

If Love and Satisfaction are what you're after,
      you may have to confront certain beliefs and myths:
            i.e., that you're not worthy of love.
                that happiness really isn't possible,
                that this relationship is "alright" until
                    the "real" one comes along.

The Truth is
      you are worthy of all the love anyone can muster
      and you're worthy of satisfaction in all of
      your relationships.

      Why would you set it up any differently?
      Why have you?

You have choices.
>   All you have to do is to look and see
>>   whether the relationship you have
>>   right now
>>>   serves you or not.

If the relationship serves you,
>   keep it and enjoy it.
If it doesn't serve you
>   either take responsibility for changing it
>>   or
>   get out of the relationship.
>   (Now that's dog doo simple!)
>   You don't need to be a martyr.

A lot of us love to play from,
>   "I'm in this relationship and I don't like it
>>>   the way it is."
Bitching is nonsense.
If you don't like the relationship
>   *choose* to do something about it.

The height of nonsense
>   is to stay in a relationship that doesn't serve you
>>   and
>>   bitch about it!

What good does it do you
>   to bitch to someone else because your relationship
>>   isn't working?
Does it serve you to bitch about your boss to your spouse?
>   or to bitch about your spouse to a friend?

When you bitch
>   your relationship stays the same
>>   you just get to go Unc for awhile.

If your relationship isn't working,
>   you're the one suffering.

You can only play from the space called, "My experience."
That's all you have.

There's nothing else on the gameboard for any of us.

If you're in a relationship
        that doesn't serve you,

        look at the lie.

You may have to take responsibility by
        re-negotiating basic agreements...
        this time based on the truth.

If your relationship isn't working,
                one of you lied.

If you told the truth and the other person lied--
        (which is usually the way you see it)--
    and
        you allowed the situation to persist,
          that too becomes a lie.
             You're in it
                     just
                         as
                            deep.

If I can't say I lied
        until you say you lied,
        neither of us
        will ever tell the truth.

If re-negotiating the agreements doesn't work,
        to clean up the relationship,
        you may have to dissolve it.
If the other party is unwilling to tell the truth,
        it doesn't serve you to maintain the relationship.

Some people are willing to live
        with the lies.
They really expect others
        to lie to them.
They persist in relationships
        based on lies.
        And then indulge
        in blame.

The most important commitment
        to make in any relationship is
            a willingness to share the truth
            whenever it becomes apparent.

With Truth comes Love.

Admit the Truth about your relationship.
        If it serves you and you have satisfaction-
                keep it the way it is.
        If it doesn't-
                take some action.

If *you* don't take action,
            nothing will happen.
Everybody keeps waiting for it all to work out for them.
        How long are you going to wait?

If you don't like the relationship

                            the way it is,
            choose to do something about it,
            because
                you'll continue to be miserable
                as long as you continue to bitch about it.

Relationships are like recordings.
        If you abuse your favorite record
                pretty soon it will get scratches.
                Finally, all you'll be able to hear are
                    the scratches,
                    and you'll end up throwing it away.

Keeping your agreements
                allows you to put your headphones on
                and
                listen to the symphony of life.

ON MARRIAGE

Marriage involves
the transformation
of me
for
the we
of us.

It means creating an environment where your partner
can be authentically real,
without fear
of repercussions
of negation
of retaliation
of judgement:

-A Free Space-

Based on love and respect and ultimate kindness.

No games.
No stamps.
No Right-Wrong.
No tally sheets.

Unfortunately, many of us have strange notions about marriage.

Since many of us felt incomplete and unworthy as
            youngsters,
we felt compelled to find someone to make us whole;
            to make us feel worthy,
            to make us feel loved.

Marriage was a means to work out a solution to a problem.
            The problem was:
                        "I'm alone."

Many of us chose to play a great fantasy.
        Some women played from
                "Some day my Prince will come...
                He'll sweep me off my feet and
                we'll live happily ever after."
        Some men played from
                "Some day I'll find my damsel-in-distress...
                I'll slay the Dragon, and I'll take my
                Beautiful Princess away and we'll live
                happily ever after."

That makes for great Disneyland material.
It just doesn't seem to work that way in
"The Real World."

After the honeymoon was over...
...or after three years
...or after seven years
...or after twenty years,
You woke up one morning,
rolled over,
took a glimpse of your Spouse,
recoiled,
and said,
"God...That's no Prince or
Princess!
I've been tricked! That's a human
being!"

It's at exactly that point that most people start giving less
to the relationship and
start saving some
for the "real" Prince or Princess
when they come along.

At first, it's,
"I'll just give 90% to this marriage
and
Save 10% for the Prince or Princess."

Then, it's
"I'll just give 75% to this marriage
and
save 25%..."

Of course, eventually it's,
"Hell, why should I give more than 40%
to this relationship? After all I'm
looking for the real Prince or Princess
to give the other 60%."

Before you know it,
you're only giving 10% to the marriage
and wondering why it's not working.

WAITING FOR IT ALL
TO HAPPEN

Everyone keeps waiting for the game to work out.
Everyone keeps waiting for the game to be won...
    without noticing that the game is already
        won, when you become "one."

It was won the instant you said, "I love you."

        That's all you had to say
            and that's all there is to say.

Marriage only becomes a chore
        when you'd rather be with
            someone-other-than-who-you're-with.
That's when the drama starts,
        when the curtain opens...

Ever notice when someone's marriage isn't working,
        they'll start sharing the drama
            about how they are the "effect" of their relationship.

        about how their spouse "is doing it to them."

It's easy to play Victim
        in marriage, because there's so much drama to be had.
If you play the Victim,
        you'll need a spouse to be a
            Persecutor or Rescuer.

People enter the union, unconsciously,
            seeking
                the other player to make the drama complete.

If the female plays Rescuer,
     and her husband is the Victim,
   it's called a
       Mommie-Atta Boy relationship.

       Mommie's take care of their Atta Boys.
       They buy their clothes,
          make their lunches,
              pat them on their Tu-Tu's and tell them
                  to be a "good-boy" at work.

       Atta Boys spend their whole lives
          being good and nice so
          Mommie will say, "Atta Boy, you did just
          fine!"

If the male plays Rescuer
    and his wife takes on the Victim role,
        it's a
           Big Daddy-Snookims relationship.

Big Daddy loves his little Snookims.
    She's his little "baby doll."
    And he proves it to the rest of the boys
        by buying her furs and diamonds and
        fancy cars.

Like Atta Boy,
    Snookims runs to Big Daddy to
    solve her problems for her--
    She being more than just a little on the
        helpless, and not too bright, side.
    And he more than willingly rescues her.

If the male plays Persecutor
  and his wife is the Victim
  it's a
    Bastard-Poor Dear relationship.

  He's the Bastard,
    always making her cower
    to his whims and desires...
        (The Poor Dear.)

She cooks, cleans, runs errands,
    and slaves for him,
    while he shows no appreciation.
    After all, she's simply fulfilling
      her "wifely" duties. (The Poor Dear.)

In social settings,
    the Poor Dear
    looks haggard, plain, and pained.
    The Bastard
      is often domineering, boisterous,
      obnoxious, talking about how he
      spends money—usually on himself.
      (The Bastard)

The reverse is where the female is Persecutor
and her husband is the Victim:
the Bitch-Nice Guy relationship.

The Bitch
rules the roost.
The Nice Guy spends his life, working like a dog,
to make her happy, which is a never-ending task.
All of the Nice Guy's friends feel sorry for him
and constantly ask themselves,
"How did a Nice Guy like Charlie get messed up
with a Bitch like that?"

One of the Nice Guy's favorite pastimes is to escape
the tirades of the Bitch,
go to the local bar,
and relate
the latest drama:
"You shoulda seen what she did to
me this time!"

This is how it all looks on the Drama Triangle:

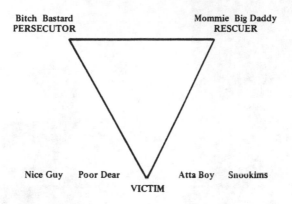

Go to any cocktail party, any bar, or any restaurant--
  and listen to the Drama.

The sad part is the lie.
        The lie is "I have no choice in the matter."
        The truth is each player has total choice.

        Bastards choose Poor Dears and Poor Dears choose Bastards.
        Bitches choose Nice Guys and Nice Guys choose Bitches.
        Mommies choose Atta Boys and Atta Boys choose Mommies.
        Daddies choose Snookims and Snookims choose Daddies.

Poor Dears get real upset if the Bastards
        treat them with respect,
        feeling, "He doesn't love me any more.
                He doesn't even care enough to beat me
                        into submission!"

If a Nice Guy
        divorces the Bitch,
        chances are real likely that
        the Nice Guy will choose another Bitch.
        (A choice, albeit an unconscious choice, but

                                no accident,
                                no coincidence.)

It's all choice.
We get what we intend to get, consciously or unconsciously.

You are responsible for your experience of your spouse.
You are the "cause" of your experience.
       Stop lying about it.

Take a look at what you're getting out of the relationship
    being what it is
      and
   tell the truth about it.

You cannot directly change your spouse,
  so stop trying.
You cannot speed the process of your spouse changing
  so stop waiting for it to happen.
You don't need your spouse,
  so stop lying about it.

You don't have to look for love outside of self
if love is coming from within you.
No relationship can suit you, if you don't feel
good about yourself.

In order for the relationship to work,
you have to accept the other person
exactly the way they are
right now.

If you find that you are unable to do so,
you'd better ask yourself why you're continuing
in the relationship.

Do you really need all that drama
to make your life seem worthwhile?

How long are you going to wait for satisfaction?

How much bitching about your spouse and your
relationship are you going to do before you admit
that the bitching is keeping you
stuck and that's how you're getting your strokes?

How long are you going to tell yourself that
you "need" the other person? You don't
need anyone. You might want to choose
to be with someone.

Notice that for a healthy relationship to last
it must come from choice, rather than need.

When you can say, "I'm complete. I'm a worthy human being
and I want to choose to be with you,"
then the relationship will work.

If you say, "I'm nothing. I need you to make
me happy," chances are it won't work.

To have a relationship work,
>you need to make an agreement
>to take total, 100% responsibility to make it work.
>If something stops working in the relationship,
>>(and you always know it immediately)
>you'll need:
>>to come totally from the truth,
>>to get off your position, and
>>to give up the Drama.
>That will bring the relationship back to
>Satisfaction.

You only get from your spouse what you're willing
>to give to your spouse.

Sometimes all the Drama is just a result of
>the inability to say,
>>>"I love you,"
>>and
>>>"I want you to love me."

By not expressing our love directly
>it becomes thwarted
>and manifests itself in other ways
>of being noticed:
>>yelling,
>>screaming,
>>accusing,
>>not talking,
>>hitting,
>>blowing up.
>>>...all unconscious pleas that say,
>>>>"Notice me. Notice me. Notice me.
>>>>Love me. Love me. Love me."

Some people feel
>they have to make war
>>to justify making love.

To end or prevent a fight,
>take a look at what's happening,
>simply acknowledge what's in it for you,
>>and
>aspect the situation from the other side
>>with love and kindness.

If you find yourself saying,
    "You don't love me enough"
look into the mirror and
repeat the message.

The purpose of marriage
        is mutual satisfaction--
                    not Drama.

Either be willing to give up the Drama
        or give up the marriage. (An act which in itself could
            create an incredible new Drama.)

        It's far
                better
                to simply give up the Drama
                and save
                the lawyer's fee.

Giving up the Drama
        just may produce you the space
                            to grow and become the "you"

        with an awareness of self that only the unity of marriage
        can provide.

ON FRIENDSHIP

A true friend
     is one who offers you
     another view of reality
        without
     making yours wrong.

The friendship is
     like an overlapping bubble of perception.
It's both a shared reality
       and the respect
     for that portion which isn't.
         That's what makes it beautiful.

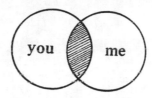

Many of us are afraid
     to share ouselves with others,
     and so we don't have deep friendships.

Sharing
     is the willingness to put out who we really are
       to others and to allow them the same potential.
It's different from
         acting out,
         dramatizing,
         or
         entertaining.
It's letting what's inside come outside.

To allow others to share themselves
     requires a safe space
       without concern about judgements,
           right-wrong,
          or
          stamp collecting
   and

   is the greatest gift of love we can offer.

ON PARENTING

Your kids are you.
> Not just when they're "good,"
> But also when they're "bad."
> They just are the way they are.
> > The rest is all your evaluation.

Take a good look into the mirror
> your kids provide you.

Children are among the most conscious
> > most loving
> > most accepting
> > most happy
> > most trusting
> > most honest
> > most intuitive
> > most wise

> > > people in the universe.

(How can we not treat them with respect
> > > and
> > > dignity?)

Notice how you want your kids to behave,
      and then be it yourself.

Kids are constantly pleading with us
      to give them responsibility:
            "Let me do it."
But because of convenience (or superiority)
      we keep "helping them," i.e. doing it for them.
      We keep them feeling inferior, helpless and
            not ok,
      which only reinforces the myth that
            they'll have to find someone to take care of them
            later in life.

By rescuing, we support the child's
                victim notions.
We get involved in the Drama constantly,
                playing persecutor or rescuer,
and then feeling victimized by our own children.

"Mommie, Johnny's hitting me again."

It takes great fortitude not to rescue,
                and to allow others to handle their own problems.

Take a look at what you're doing
        for
                your kids.
Are you getting them up in the morning,
                and bitching when they're late for breakfast?
                Let them get an alarm clock and take responsibility
                        for getting up themselves.

Are you making certain that they're doing their homework?
Making certain that they are doing their homework problems
        right?
Making certain that they get good grades?

Whose homework is it?
Whose grades are on the report card?
Who's going to take your place when independent
learning is required?

Are you doing their cooking, setting the table,
doing their wash, driving them around, doing their
dishes, cleaning their rooms, planning their school
activities, defending them at school?

How long are you going to do "for"
        rather than "with"?

Of course, age is a factor.
        You may have to walk your
        two year old across a busy intersection
        whereas, it's not appropriate for a fourteen year old.

At some point,
    you have to give up rescuing
    and allow your children to take responsibility
        for their lives.

To let your kids take responsibility
    is to allow them to feel good about themselves.

It's no wonder that so many children
    grow up, leave home, and search for someone
        to take care of them.
    Then when that doesn't work,
        they come home and ask for more rescuing.

Why not let your children
    take responsibility
    by guiding them, pointing out what they might have done
        if they failed.
    You need to give them the awareness that you have
    confidence in their ability to solve their own problems
        and
    to run their own lives successfully.

The purpose of a family
    is to create a non-judgmental atmosphere
    where the individuals can grow
        through love and acceptance.

The family can provide
    the one safe space where you can
    truly be yourself and can share yourself
    with others.

Each member of the family can
    learn from every other member.
    No matter how young,
    children provide us with a blueprint for living.
Christ was accurate
    when He said that we must all
        become as small children to enter the kingdom
            of Heaven.

We need to learn from our children,
the sense of wonder,
the joy of creating,
the act of experiencing,
the freedom of
emotional expression,
the wonder and
beauty of love.

And they need to learn from us
how to create a world
that will allow them to continue to be
who they are
and to consciously experience what they're
experiencing, Right Now.

In order for this to happen
we need to create an environment where the learning
can take place...a trusting, non-threatening environment.
For many parents,
the hitting and yelling diminishes
when we notice that there are other
ways to get close.

We need to become the parents
we vowed we would be,
when we were children.
That would break the cycle
that has been repeated for generations.

The ultimate gift
you can give your children
is to allow them to know who you are,
and to allow them the freedom to be who they are.

ON THERAPY

In therapy,
     you'll get well to the extent
        that you're willing to tell the truth
     about how you set up your life the way it is.

Imagine going to a physician with a pain in your arm,
     and being unwilling to say where you hurt.
     "Doctor, doctor, I'm sick! I hurt!"
        "Where are you experiencing pain?"
     "I won't tell you!"

It's like sitting in the physician's office
     hoping to be asked if your arm hurts.

Sounds ridiculous with a physician,
     and yet it happens all the time with therapists.

In order for therapy to work
     you have to be willing to face your life,
     the way you set it up
     and then be willing to share the truth with your
     therapist.

Therapy works
     when it promotes
        sharing the Truth.

When someone
     with incredible acts and tapes
     goes to a therapist for "help", it may be a sad joke.

Let's say the client has everything figured out.
     He should be able to put all the pieces together.
     He says, "Doctor what's my problem?"
          There he is asking the therapist the question
          that only he can answer.

What does the therapist do?
     It depends on whether the therapist is ethical.

It is the height of being unethical
to keep the client in a Victim position,
     to buy the client's lies;
          to continue to Rescue week after week, and
          to charge money for it.

The client,
     having no intention of changing,
     looks for a therapist who will support Victim notions.
     Unwilling to confront the uncomfortableness
     that significant change will necessitate,
          continues to lie to the therapist and self.

     Eventually, feeling like, "this is getting me nowhere,"
          he complains bitterly about the loss of money
          and that the therapist, "didn't help me."

The client continues feeling miserable,
     only now feels justified, (after all he went for counseling),
          in maintaining the problematic behavior.
     Then, if all else fails, the search for the magic
          therapist or "cure" continues.

     The joke is on the client
     and the punchline is, "guess who's still miserable?"

The Therapist
  having no intention of really confronting
  the client with the responsibilities of having
    created such a life drama,
    continues to "play it safe"
    through being
      analytical and
        detached. And by
         reflecting
          and listening.
The Therapist
  never once has to ask,
    "Why did you set it up that way?"
    "What are you getting out of it?"
    "When are you going to do something about it?"

The joke is on the Therapist,
  because a therapist can't help anyone
  and the punchline is
    "I've tried so hard, and he never followed my advice
    or did what I told him to, etc., etc..."

The purpose of therapy
  is to increase the client's level of satisfaction
  by promoting the individual's own potential for problem-
  solving
    not
  to make the individual "feel better"
  when the good feelings stop with the weekly sessions.

Many therapists
        have "professional" wired up with "passive."
        Some feel that if they can find the appropriate label
        for the behavior they won't have to deal with it.

One of the major issues
        confronting the therapeutic relationship
        is promoting health
                        rather than
                                conformity,
        to a psychologically fragmented and ill society.

If to be "well" is to be "normal"
        therapy should not be part of the process.

If as therapists we teach clients to suppress,
                rather than dealing with or allowing
                the completion of the experience,
we are complicating the process of growth.
                Completion cures.

Promoting the sharing of all those things
        the client has been unwilling or unable to share in the past,
        allows the client control over those aspects of his life.

Promoting "twenty questions"
        is to fall into the trap of the mind
        and to enhance resistance.

Therapy should encompass
                        a discovery process.
        The discovery of self.
        The discovery that one's problems are opportunities
                and abilities.
        The discovery that the truth works.
        The discovery that the self is lovable and perfect
                and worthy.
        The discovery that life doesn't have to get bad
                to get
                        better.

THE GURU REVISITED

The Truthseeker sat confused and frustrated. After a
        long pause, he said,
                "I just don't understand any of this."

"You probably never will," the Guru stated in a knowing,
compassionate way. "You can never understand the Truth.
        You
                just are
                        the Truth.
        Understanding, evaluating, and judging are all
                senseless activities. The Truth is You Are.
Your experience is your reality
        and
your reality is a composite of your experience.

We all live in separate realities. The only one you can
        ever be sure of is your own.

When something occurs in your experience that you don't
like, you can blame something or someone else.
        You can be the effect of your experience
                or
        you can take responsibility for your experience.
Notice that you've been the cause of your experience all along.
And if there's any change to be made, you're the one who's
        going to make it.

One of the major obstacles for getting your life to
        work the way you want it to is your
                own mind.

Your mind made recordings so you could learn and survive.
Yet your mind is like a plane with no pilot.
It goes unconscious whenever threatened; even though
        sometimes it's totally inappropriate.

You become unconscious when an association with a past
        experience is triggered.
This is especially true of negative events.

Because your spiritual nature is one of being completely
        ethical,
        everytime you act unethically, you pay
        yourself back by giving up your
            aliveness and satisfaction.

    If you tell lies to yourself,
        you live a life of frustration.
    If you tell lies to others,
        you create drama and dissatisfaction.

And yet, you always know the truth
        because it's your experience.

To gain the satisfaction and inner peace
        you've searched so many years to find,
            stop searching and start living.
            Realize that satisfaction is a result of
                acceptance,
                    of being conscious,
                        of sharing yourself,
                        and
                        of serving others.

Life will continue to flow smoothly when you:
  give up trying to be someone you're not,
  stop bitching and lying,
  establish where you want to go and what
        you want to have, and then just begin the
        process, without waiting for it to happen
        to you, or for someone else to do it *for* you."

The Truthseeker looked up, blinked his eyes, and said:

  "Yes,
        I think
              I'm starting to see it.
                    I understand now...
                          I'm the one who..."

The Truthseeker stopped
        as he watched the Guru
              become a mirror
                    reflecting his own image.

     Knowingly, the Guru smiled
                          and
                                simply
                                      disappeared.

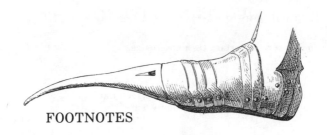

FOOTNOTES

p. 93   *Matthew* 7:12.

p. 97   Stephen Karpman. "Fairy Tales and Script Drama Analysis." *T.A. Bulletin* 7:26 (April, 1968) 39-43.

p. 111   Muriel James and Dorothy Jongeward. *Born to Win.* Menlo Park, California: Addison-Wesley, 1971.

p. 119   Eric Berne. *Games People Play.* New York: Grove Press, 1964.

p. 146   *Webster's Seventh New Collegiate Dictionary.* Springfield, Mass.: G. & C. Merriam Co., 1967, p. 626.

p. 163   Lao Tsu. *The Way of Life According to Laotzu,* translated by Witter Bynner. New York: Capricorn Books, 1962.

p. 171   David Campbell. *If You Don't Know Where You're Going, You'll Probably End Up Somewhere Else.* Niles, Illinois: Argus Communications, 1974.

p. 195   Everett Shostrum and James Kavanaugh. *Between Man and Woman.* Los Angeles: Nash Publishing, 1971. Compare with names these authors provide for relationships: Mother/Son, Daddy/Doll, Bitch/Nice Guy, Master/Slave. In the interest of equally negative sexism, these names were altered somewhat for this book. Shostrum and Kavanaugh provide an excellent instrument called the "Love Attraction Inventory."

QUOTES TO LIVE BY....

"Imagination is more important than knowledge."

--Albert Einstein

"Happiness is not in our circumstances, but in ourselves.
It is not something we see, like a rainbow, or feel, like
the heat of a fire. Happiness is something we are."

--John B. Sheerin

"A man should never be ashamed to say he has been wrong,
which is but saying, in other words, that he is wiser today
than he was yesterday."

--Alexander Pope

"One who fears, limits his activities. Failure is only the
opportunity to more intelligently begin again."

--Henry Ford

"Demanding and rejecting, criticizing and judging, 'righting'
and 'wronging' are the sickness of the mind. To be free
of distorted perceptions, see the chains of addictive patterns
that dominate our consciousness and make our lives a battle.
Our perception of others is only your projection of fears
and desires for ourselves."

--Kenneth Keyes

"The higher the degree of responsibility, the greater the
motivation."

--Kingman Brewster, Jr.

"The only people who don't have problems are the people who
don't do anything."

--Kemmons Wilson,
Founder of Holiday Inns, Inc.

"Those who would give up essential liberty to purchase a little
temporary safety deserve neither liberty nor safety."

--Benjamin Franklin

"Every individual has a place to fill in the world and is
important in some respect, whether he chooses to be so or not."

--Nathaniel Hawthorne

"Without going outside, you may know the whole world. Without
looking through the window, you may see the ways of heaven.
The farther you go, the less you know."

--Lao Tzu

"No persons are more frequently wrong, than those who will not
admit that they are wrong."

--Francois Due de la Rochefoucauld

"The condition of alienation, of being asleep, of being
unconscious, of being out of one's mind, is the condition
of normal man."

--R. D. Laing

"We have forty million reasons for failure, but not a single
excuse."

–Rudyard Kipling

"I am an optimist. It does not seem much use to be anything
else."

--Winston Churchill

"Man is never so attached to anything as his own suffering."

--Gurdjieff

"Truth--The Beginning.
Peace--The Meaning.
Love--The Essence."

--Kriensky

"Face the simple fact before it becomes involved.
Solve the small problem before it becomes big.
The most involved fact in the world
Could have been faced when it was simple.
The biggest problem in the world
Could have been solved when it was small.

The simple fact that he finds no problem big
Is a sane man's prime achievement."

--Lao Tzu

"You can never get enough of what you don't need to make
you happy."

–Eric Hoffer

"The statement of our consciousness is the extent to which
we joyfully produce results...in our own lives and the lives
of others, in the environment of this planet we share."

--Stewart Emery

"Happiness? It is an illusion to think that more comfort
means more happiness. Happiness comes of the capacity to
feel deeply, to enjoy simply, to think freely, to risk life,
to be needed."

--Storm Jameson

"If you ever find happiness by hunting for it, you will find
it as the old woman did her lost spectacles--on her nose all
the time."

--Josh Billings

"Wealth consists not in having great possessions, but in having few wants."

--Epicurus

"Life is not having and a getting, but a being and becoming."

--Matthew Arnold

"In the province of the main, what one believes to be true, either is true or becomes true within certain limits to be found experientially and experimentally. These limits are further beliefs to be transcended. In the province of the mind, there are no limits."

--John C. Lilly

"Responsibility is a unique concept. It can only reside and inhere in a single individual. You may share it with others, but your portion is not diminished. You may delegate it, but it is still with you. You may disclaim it, but you cannot divest yourself of it."

--Admiral Rickover

"The price of greatness is responsibility."

--Winston Churchill

"If you manage people by letting them alone,
Ghosts of the dead shall not haunt you.

Fail to honor people,
They fail to honor you."

--Lao Tzu

"Only a fish can do an autobiography of a fish."

--Carl Sandburg

"Love joins our present with the past and the future."

--Kahlil Gibran

"And only when we are no longer afraid do we begin to live in every experience, painful or joyous; to live in gratitude for every moment, to live abundantly."

–Dorothy Thompson

"The clearer I perceive that which is True, the less reasoning, judging, arguing I can do."

--Angelus Silesius

"It is better to do nothing than to do what is wrong. For whatever you do, you do to yourself. See what is. See what is not. Follow the true way. Rise."

--Buddha

"From without, no wonderful effect is wrought within ourselves unless some interior, responding wonder meets it."

--Herman Melville

"The Universe is not to be narrowed down to the limits of the understanding, which has been men's practice up to now, but the understanding must be stretched and enlarged to take in the image of the universe as it is discovered."

--Francis Bacon

"...it is the soul that thirsts for truth. The intellect only to satiate its fascination."

--Ram Dass

"It's not where you're going, it's where you're coming from."

-Nathaniel Lande

"You become what you behold."

--William Blake

"If you never assume importance, you never lost it."

--Lao Tzu

"When at last we understand how we do it to ourselves and create the world we experience, we can live as awakening life."

--Kenneth Keyes

"If you don't know where you're going, you can't get there. And you can't get anywhere until you know who you are."

--Seneca

"Consciousness is the totality beyond space-time-what may in essence be the real "I". We have come to know that consciousness and energy are one; that all of space-time is constructed by consciousness...Therefore, our full energies are devoted to the study of consciousness. There is no other task. Working toward a transformation in consciousness is the only game in town."

--Bob Toben

"We are what we think. All that we are arises with our thoughts. With our thoughts we make the world."

--Buddha

"The individual is responsible for what happens in the future, no matter what has happened in the past...and as long as people are bound by the past, they are not free to respond to the needs and aspirations of others in the present."

--Thomas Harris

"The wise man looks into space, and does not regard the
small as too little, not the great as too big; for he knows
that there is no limit to dimension."

--Lao Tzu

"People are always blaming circumstances for what they are.
I don't believe in circumstances. The people who get on
in this world are the people who get up and look for the
circumstances they want, and if they can't find them, make
them."

–George Bernard Shaw

"Something began me and it had no beginning; something will
end me, and it has no end."

--Carl Sandburg

"Mistaking the false for the true, and the true for the
false, you overlook the heart and fill yourself with desire.
See the false as false, the true as true, look into your
heart. Follow your nature.

The fool who knows he is a fool is that much wiser. The
fool who thinks he is wise is a fool indeed."

--Buddha

Recommended Reading

David Augsburger, *Caring Enough to Confront;* Regal.

Richard B. Austin, Jr., *How To Make It With Another Person;* MacMillan.

Richard Bach, *Illusions--the Adventures of a Reluctant Messiah;* Delacorte Press.

Beier & Valens, *People Reading;* Stein & Day.

Eric Berne, *Games People Play;* Grove Press.
Sex in Human Loving; Simon & Schuster.
What Do You Say After You Say Hello? Grove Press.

Nathaniel Branden, *Breaking Free;* Bantam.

Claude M. Bristol, *The Magic of Believing;* Pocket Books.

Harry Browne, *How I Found Freedom in an Unfree World;* Avon.

Martin Buber, *I and Thou;* Charles Scribner's Sons.

Richard M. Bucke, *Cosmic Consciousness;* Dutton & Company.

David Campbell, *If You Don't Know Where You're Going, You'll Probably End Up Somewhere Else;* Argus Communications.

Carlos Castaneda, *The Teachings of Don Juan;* Pocket Books.
A Separate Reality; Pocket Books.
Journey to Ixtlan; Pocket Books.
Tales of Power; Simon & Schuster.

Ram Dass, *Be Here Now;* Lama Foundation.
The Only Dance There Is; Anchor Books.

C. D. Deshmukh, *Sparks of the Truth: From the Dissertations of Meher Baba;* Sheriar Press.

Wayne W. Dyer, *Your Erroneous Zones;* Funk & Wagnalls.

Steward Emery, *Actualizations--You Don't Have to Rehearse to Be Yourself;* Doubleday Dolphin.

Victor E. Frankl, *Man's Search for Meaning;* Pocket Books.

Frederick Franck, *The Book of Angelus Silesius;* Vintage Press.

Carl Frederick, *est: Playing the Game the New Way;* Dell.

Erick Fromm, *The Art of Loving;* Bantam.
            Escape from Freedom; Farrar & Reinhart.

Kahill Gibran, *The Prophet;* Alfred A. Knopf.

Jerr Greenwald, *Be the Person You Were Meant to Be;* Dell.

G. I. Gurdjieff, *All and Everything;* Dutton.
            Meetings with Remarkable Men; Dutton.

Thomas Harris, *I'm OK, You're OK;* Avon.

Robert A. Heinlein, *Stranger in a Strange Land;* Putnam.

Herman Hesse, *Journey to the East;* Noonday.
            Siddhartha; New Directions.
            Steppenwolf; Holt Rhinehart.

Yoel Hoffman, *The Sound of One Hand;* Basic Books.

Aldous Huxley, *Island;* Holt Rhinehart.

Laura Huxley, *This Timeless Moment;* Holt Rhinehart.

James & Jongeward, *Born to Win;* Addison Wesley.

Muriel James, *The OK Boss;* Addison Wesley.

William James, *The Varieties of Religious Experience;* Modern Library.

Arthur Janov, *The Primal Scream;* Putnam.

Ceasar Johnson, *To See a World in a Grain of Sand;* C. R.
     Gibson Company.

David W. Johnson, *Reaching Out;* Prentice Hall.

Sidney M. Jourard, *Disclosing Man to Himself;* Van Nostrand-Reinhold.
            The Transparent Self; Van Nostrand-Reinhold.

Philip Kapleau, *The Three Pillars of Zen;* Harper & Row.

Sam Keen, *To a Dancing God;* Harper & Row.

Ken Keyes, *Handbook to Higher Consciousness;* Living Love.
        Loving Your Body; Living Love.
        Taming Your Mind; Living Love.

Ken Keyes with Bruce Burkan, *How to Make Your Life Work;*
    Living Love.

Shelton B. Kopp, *Guru;* Bantam.

J. Krishnamurti, *You Are the World;* Harper & Row.
        Commentaries on Living; Harper & Row.
        Education and the Significance of Life; Harper & Row.

R. D. Laing, *The Divided Self;* Pantheon.
        The Politics of Experience; Ballantine.
        Knots; Vintage.
        Facts of Life; Pantheon.

Jess Lair, *I Ain't Much Baby But I'm All I Got;* Fawcett Crest.
        I Ain't Well–But I Sure Am Better; Fawcett Crest.

Lao Tzu, *Tao Te Ching;* Blackney-Translator.

George Leonard, *The Ultimate Athlete;* Viking Press.

John C. Lilly, *The Center of the Cyclone;* Julian Press.
        Simulations of God: the Science of Belief;
    Simon & Schuster.

Maxwell Maltz, *Psycho-Cybernetics: Creative Living for
    Today;* Pocket Books.

Abraham Maslow, *The Farther Reaches of Human Consciousness;*
    Harper.
        Motivation and Personality; Harper.

Rollo May, *Love and Will;* Norton.
        The Courage to Create; Bantam.

Meher Baba, *God Speaks: the Theme of Creation and Its Purpose;*
    Dodd Mead & Company.
        Discourses. Vols. 1-4, Dodd Mead & Company.

Peter McWilliams, *I Love Therefore I Am;* Versemonger Press.

Jeffrey Mishlove, *The Roots of Consciousness;* Random House.

Gerald I. Nierenberg and Henry H. Calero, *Meta-Talk;* Pocket Books.

Ken Olson, *The Art of Hanging Loose in an Uptight World;*
    Fawcett Crest.

Robert Ornstein, *The Nature of Human Consciousness;* Viking Press.

P. D. Ouspensky; *In Search of the Miraculous;* Harcourt Brace.
    The Psychology of Man's Possible Evolution;
Harcourt Brace.
    A New Model of the Universe; Harcourt Brace.
    The Fourth Way; Knopf.

Joseph C. Pearce, *The Crack in the Cosmic Egg;* Pocket Books.

Fritz Perls, *In and Out the Garbage Pail;* Bantam.
    Gestalt Therapy Verbatim; Bantam.

Robert Persig, *Zen and the Art of Motorcycle Maintenance;*
    Bantam.

Frieda Porat with Karen Meyers, *Changing Your Life Style;* Bantam.

Swami Prabhavananda, *The Sermon on the Mount According to
    Vedanta;* Mentor.

Hugh Prather, *I Touch the Earth, the Earth Touches Me;* Real
    People Press.
    Notes to Myself; Real People Press.

Tom Robbins, *Even Cowgirls Get the Blues;* Houghton Mifflin.

Rogers & Stevens, *Person to Person: The Problem of Being;*
    Real People Press.

Carl Rogers, *On Becoming a Person;* Real People Press.

Elizabeth Kubler-Ross, *On Death and Dying;* MacMillan.

William Schultz, *Joy: Expanding Human Awareness;* Grove Press.

Susan Polis Schutz and Nancy Hoffman, *I Care About Your
    Happiness: Quotations From the Love Letters of Kahlil
    Gibran and Mary Haskell;* Blue Mountain Arts.

Susan Polis Schutz, *I Want to Laugh, I Want to Cry;* Blue
    Mountain Arts.
        Come Into the Mountains, Dear Friend; Blue
    Mountain Arts.
        The Language of Friendship; Blue Mountain Arts.

David Seabury, *The Art of Selfishness;* Cornerstone Library.

Merle Shain, *Some Men Are More Perfect Than Others;* Bantam.

Harold Sherman, *How to Take Yourself Apart and Put Yourself
    Together Again;* Fawcett Crest.

Everett Shostrum, *Man the Manipulator;* Bantam.

Adam Smith, *Powers of the Mind;* Ballantine.

Manuel J. Smith, *When I Say No, I Feel Guilty;* Dial Press.

Claude Steiner, *Scripts People Live;* Grove Press.

David Stuart, *Alan Watts;* Chilton Book Company.

D. T. Suzuki, *What is Zen;* Harper & Row.

Bob Toben, *Space-Time and Beyond;* Dutton.

Alvin Toffler, *Future Shock;* Random House.

David S. Viscott, *How to Make Winning Your Lifestyle;* Dell.
        How to Live With Another Person; Pocket Books.

Frank Walters, *Book of the Hopi;* Ballantine.

Alan Watts, *This Is It;* Random House.
        The Book: On the Taboo Against Knowing Who You Are;
    Random House.
        Psychotherapy East and West; Ballantine.

FOR YOUR INFORMATION

A GREAT BUSINESS GUIDE

☞ G. Michael Durst's second book, **Management by Responsibility,** is now available. This book puts into a business framework the principles and philosophy of **Napkin Notes. Management by Responsibilty** offers a complete description of the levels of psychological development, including specific ways to improve your management style and effectiveness through becoming more self-actualized.

As a reference guide or an introduction to management, this stimulating book is a **MUST.**

YOU ARE INVITED TO ATTEND

☞ The dynamic seminar entitled Management by Responsibilty has been attended by thousands of employees of Fortune 500 companies and government agencies throughout the country. This seminar presents the best of the MBR philosophy which is wholistic in its approach towards management. Recognizing that productivity and effectiveness are an outgrowth of employee satisfaction and are in direct proportion to the responsibility assumed, MBR teaches responsible leadership and provides a management style that is both accountable and effective.

This is the management course that works!

MBR AVAILABLE IN VIDEO AND AUDIO CASSETTE FORMAT

☞ The video series of Management by Responsibility has captured Dr. G.M. Durst's unique ability to express complex terms and theories through a simple and straightforward approach. Through the use of facilitators, the video tapes are correlated with exercises which actively challenge participants to expand their understanding of MBR. It is now possible for everyone in an organization to be exposed to one of the most dynamic philosophies of management available today.

This can mean a broad expansion toward creating a more satisfying and effective working environment.

☞ For further information regarding Dr. Durst's books, seminars, video cassette programs, or to inquire about becoming a licensed facilitator, call or write today:

Training Systems, Inc.
P.O. Box 788
Evanston, Illinois 60204
312.864.8710